HEALING CHILD TRAUMA THROUGH RESTORATIVE PARENTING

A Model for Supporting Children and Young People

Dr Chris Robinson and Terry Philpot

Foreword by Andrew Constable
and Karen Mitchell-Mellor

Jessica Kingsley *Publishers*
London and Philadelphia

First published in 2016
by Jessica Kingsley Publishers
73 Collier Street
London N1 9BE, UK
and
400 Market Street, Suite 400
Philadelphia, PA 19106, USA

www.jkp.com

Library of Congress Cataloging in Publication Data
Names: Robinson, Chris, 1962- author. | Philpot, Terry, author.
Title: Healing child trauma through restorative parenting : a model for
   supporting children and young people / Chris Robinson and Terry Philpot.
Description: London ; Philadelphia : Jessica Kingsley Publishers, [2016] |
   Includes bibliographical references and index.
Identifiers: LCCN 2015050739 | ISBN 9781849056991 (alk. paper)
Subjects: LCSH: Parent and child. | Psychic trauma in children. |
   Parenting--Psychological aspects. | Child welfare.
Classification: LCC BF723.P25 R625 2016 | DDC 649/.154--dc23 LC record
available at http://lccn.loc.gov/2015050739

British Library Cataloguing in Publication Data
A CIP catalogue record for this book is available from the British Library

ISBN 978 1 84905 699 1
eISBN 978 1 78450 215 7

Printed and bound in Great Britain

To the children – from whom I am always learning.
(Chris Robinson)

To Bob Holman, a true champion for parents and children, for many years of friendship, in admiration and affection.
(Terry Philpot)

CONTENTS

FOREWORD

This is the most detailed explanation of the Restorative Parenting®
programme.[1] The concept is based on the idea of creating a re-
parenting environment, to restore the psychological deficits which
children have suffered at the hands of their own parents and often
of other adults. It was originally developed by Halliwell Homes (see
pages 125–126).

The children with whom Halliwell Homes works have suffered
trauma, aggravated often by frequent breakdown in placements,
such as fostering, residential care and adoption. Most of all this has
led them to distrust adults. Restoring that trust (or, in many cases,
creating it for the first time) is the task of restorative parenting.

Chris Robinson and Terry Philpot, in what is a comprehensive
description of our work, describe the backgrounds from which the
children come; their lives before care; the cause and nature of trauma;
and the attitudes that this has created in them. They look at the
impact which sexual (often combined with physical) abuse has on
children's psychological and emotional development.

Of course, each child is different and the programme treats them
individually, seeking to treat the whole child. How this is done is
explained in this book. This programme is about the creation of
therapeutic living space; the role of the therapeutic parent; how clinical
knowledge of a child can inform her long-term lifestyle choices;
the role of education, both through Halliwell's own schools, and
mainstream schools; and issues of staff recruitment and the qualities
they need for the work, and their training, qualification and retention.

---

1   Restorative Parenting is a registered trademark of Halliwell Homes. We
     have only included the symbol on the first appearance of the term for ease
     of reading.

Halliwell has developed restorative parenting, but its concepts and principles are applicable to all children of the kind described here. It is a clinical programme, but also a humanistic one. It is based on optimism, positing not only that each child who has been injured through abuse should have the opportunity to recover, but suggesting how restorative parenting can help them to realise that opportunity.

Andrew Constable and Karen Mitchell-Mellor,
Directors, Halliwell Homes

A NOTE AND ACKNOWLEDGEMENTS

The names of the children and young people mentioned in this book have, of course, been changed, as well as any details that might have identified them.

For ease of reading we have referred to children in the feminine form ('she') and all adults in the masculine form ('he') unless, of course, we are referring to specific cases and situations.

Writing this book has been very much a joint enterprise. We have spent many days in discussion, exchanging ideas and opinions, both as to subject matter and the shape of the book. During this process Terry Philpot wrote the text for each chapter, which we both then read, and Chris Robinson made comments, additions, amendments and deletions, from which the final text emerged.

This process was the same with regard to Chapter 7 on education, where Terry Philpot worked with Matthew Hargreaves, director of education, Halliwell Homes, but Chris Robinson also made comments and amendments.

We are grateful to Georgina Speake, assistant psychologist, Halliwell Homes, for the help with Figure 1.1.

CHAPTER 1

Children in Care

What Is Care and Why Are the Children There?

The experience of people who were looked after in care homes as children has been the focus of much public interest and concern. High profile enquiries into historical allegations of child abuse have resulted in shocking reports of institutions which have not only failed to provide adequate care, but have allowed and supported practices which have further harmed already damaged and vulnerable children. Stories of sexual and physical abuse, neglect and exploitation, often spanning many years, have become sadly commonplace.

The personal stories behind such headlines reflect lives blighted by the enduring emotional and psychological legacy of abuse, which for many children compounded earlier traumas of rejection and abandonment.

Children enter the care system because of failures in parenting. They have often been severely neglected, emotionally and physically, and many have suffered sexual abuse and cruelty. Exposure to parental mental illness, family breakdowns, alcoholism, drug addiction and violence are common experiences in the documented stories of children going through care proceedings. Removing a child from such experiences to protect them from further harm, and in some cases to save their lives, is a necessary and vital step.

This physical act of rescue can be seen as both an emergency response and a last resort, but social workers and other involved professionals know that taking a child away from the family is not just the 'something that needs to be done' which occupies the headline writers and politicians. The immediate focus of concern around the child at the time of removal is usually very high, but it begins to fade quickly once the deed is done. It is as if, once rescued, there is an assumption that the child is now somehow safe and the level of concern can be relaxed.

Of course, the stories of survivors tell us, and the inquiries mentioned above reveal, that removing a child from an abusive situation is not always the act of rescue it is intended to be. In the worst cases, the child can be saved from one abusive situation only to be handed into another.

In reality the rescue of a child from the harm of failed parenting is not an event that ends with a child protected. It is the beginning of a process that must carry on long after the immediate concerns have passed and, to be effective, that process must translate the initial act of rescue into sustainable, long-term recovery.

This belief that the rescue of the child is an end in itself is, maybe, the most damaging to the care system because residential care has so poor a public image. This is a misleading view of children in care and the care system, which tends to paint both as uniformly bad.

In fact, as at 31 March 2015, there were 69,540 children and young people in care in England (68,800 in the previous year). Of the total number, 52,050 (75%) were in foster care; 6570 (9%) were living in secure units, children's homes or hostels; 3510 (5%) with their parents; 3320 (5%) were placed for adoption; 2280 (3%) had another placement in the community; and 1750 (3%) were living in residential schools or other residential settings. Of these children and young people, 38,530 (55%) were boys and 31,010 (45%) were girls (Coram BAAF, 2015).

The preference for children who are looked-after is for fostering, but there are those whose emotional and behavioural difficulties do not allow this kind of placement. There are some other children and young people who do not wish to be adopted or to go into foster care, or they are too old for the options to be considered.

The main reason why children are taken into care is abuse or neglect, with other reasons including a parent's illness or disability; a child's disability; a dysfunctional family; absent parents; low income; and family stress.

Sometimes an over-emphasis by a commissioning local authority on the cost of a placement rather than the benefit to the child means that a child is moved to a less satisfactory placement. An important criterion that the local authority applies here is – can we afford it? If we look at the damage to the child of inappropriate care and, later, to the effect that unhealed trauma may have on that child and her adult relationships, and the wider society, the criterion, in our view, ought to be – can we not afford it?

The causes and effects of trauma

The types of trauma a child can experience are many and varied; as to some extent are the means by which the trauma can come about. In this book we are concerned with the trauma children suffer as a result of catastrophic failures in parenting, such that they can no longer live with the very people who, more than any other, are supposed to provide them with basic care and protection. Many of these children will also have suffered abuse, sexual, physical and emotional, and some will have not, but all have suffered the trauma of parental rejection. These are children who cannot live with their parents and families and who, so far, have found no place which can help them recover from the enormity of that exclusion.

A child who has experienced such profound trauma is one to whom extraordinarily damaging things have happened. Fundamentally, their ability to form trusting relationships at any level has been broken.

Restorative parenting recognises, as a core principle, that children who have been subject to abuse, neglect and parental rejection have suffered trauma. The nature and extent of the trauma our children have suffered is not discrete or fixed in time and place. These children have suffered chronic adversity, rejection and abuse, some of them over many years.

The commonly used language of trauma is adapted from the literature on post-traumatic stress disorder (PTSD) and may not be helpful as it fails to capture the pervasive nature of abuse and rejection, which for the children we work with is often a pernicious process rather than a single event or series of events which can be reduced to discrete episodes (van der Kolk, 2003).

Contemporary research is increasingly moving away from narrow models of neurology which link childhood trauma to discrete changes in brain anatomy (Evans and Kim, 2012). The chronic trauma of child abuse, neglect and parental rejection is increasingly recognised as creating a more general syndrome of toxic childhood stress (TCS), which impacts on developing biological systems in diffuse and enduring ways (Evans and Kim, 2012). These ideas are not entirely new. Nearly 20 years ago the Adverse Childhood Experiences (ACE) Study described multiple stresses that can induce a toxic stress response: child abuse or neglect, parental substance abuse and maternal depression (Felitti *et al.*, 1998).

However, what is increasingly recognised is the pervasive impact of such abuses and how they can profoundly influence the way in which a child interacts with and experiences the world around her.

What is now generally referred to as TCS is characterised by the disruption of brain circuitry and other organic and metabolic systems during childhood development, resulting in changes (both anatomical and physiological/structural and functional) that are precursors for impairments in learning and behaviour, and chronic stress-related physical and mental illness (Shonkoff and Garner, 2012).

The response of a child to environmental and social stressors has been reported to be associated with their predictive adaptive response (PAR) (Bateson *et al.*, 2014; Rosenström *et al.*, 2015). The PAR is thought to drive an optimal developmental path based on current environmental conditions, which subsequently produces stable developmental differences in behaviour (Wolf *et al.*, 2008). This occurs because current surroundings provide the child with a prediction of circumstances – an in-built weather forecast of conditions that are likely to occur in the future (for example, needs not being met).

When children have been exposed to TCS, their reactions to subsequent stress stimuli become programmed to start quicker, to last longer and to be of greater intensity (Carroll *et al.*, 2013). Consequently, children who have suffered TCS have a substantially reduced ability to regulate physiological, emotional and behavioural responding, and an increased likelihood of encountering chronic stress-related health problems (Carroll *et al.*, 2013).

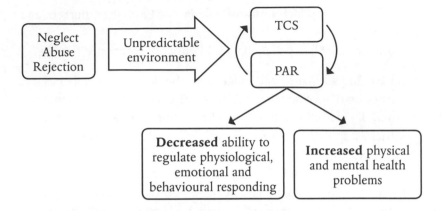

Figure 1.1: The interplay between toxic childhood stress (TCS) and predictive adaptive response (PAR) in relation to childhood trauma.

While the research into toxic childhood stress and its harmful general impact is compelling, it is also true that just as there are no typical children, there are no typical abused or rejected children. It is important to understand how the experience of trauma can have an impact upon children, but it is almost equally important to be aware that each child is unique and there is no linear causal pathway between the experience of trauma and the way a child then experiences the world.

The effects of the trauma of abuse and rejection are profound, but growth and development are continuous, interactive processes. What has happened to a child evokes different reactions in each victim, and trauma differs from child to child in its effects. What we do know is that the effects will be deeply damaging and that the help leading to healing will last a long time and is on one level subtle, sophisticated, sensitive and highly skilled, but also as basic and fundamental as the damage it seeks to correct, as this book will demonstrate.

The children about whom this book is concerned are those who have experienced a variety of causes which induce developmental trauma, all of which arise from a catastrophic breakdown in parenting – in some cases, no parenting at all because the parents are absent. Thus, we are talking about sexual and physical abuse, emotional and physical neglect, rejection, abandonment, exposure to severe domestic abuse, parental misuse of drugs and alcohol and any other factors which result in a failure of basic care, nurture and protection.

Koomar (2009) explains that children who experience trauma:

> have impairments, particularly in the area of social and emotional development… The social effects of early trauma may include difficulty or inability to develop and maintain friendships; alienation from or oppositional behaviour toward parents, caregivers and authority figures; and difficulty with trust, intimacy and affection. These children also may lack empathy, compassion and remorse; abuse substances; and perpetuate the cycle of maltreatment and attachment disorder in their own children when they reach adulthood.

The children who enter the Restorative Parenting programme are among the most severely affected of all those in care and demand highly specialised help. Yet many of the children will have previously been placed in unsatisfactory residential care and some in foster placements (even several) which have broken down because the placement was not able to deal with the severity of the child's needs and situation. Behind that definition of the children about whom we write lies a history and complexity which offers a context for the work of restorative parenting.

The effects of developmental trauma are deep and wide-ranging. Neglect and abuse, be it emotional, physical or sexual, have their impact on the body, on the developing physical as well as emotional and psychological systems. We have tended to think that it is the brain only which suffers developmentally from abuse, but it is the whole self, physically and psychically, where the impacts are felt by such profound stress. The cognitive, psychological and emotional are intertwined, and it follows that, to be effective, a recovery programme must operate across and between these interconnected levels. We cannot separate good nurture, welfare, good physical health and healthy emotional development. This means that, in working with these children, we have to take account of the totality of their lived experience; thus, everything that impacts on them deserves attention.

The Restorative Parenting recovery programme aims to help those children who not only cannot live with their birth families, but whom mainstream foster and residential care has also been unable to help.

Sometimes a child can be taken into mainstream public care as a necessary act of protection, only for the experience to increase her problems. Initial placements often prove unsuitable for a variety of reasons, not least because it is practically very difficult to maintain unused capacity in an overstretched care system. Decisions of where to place children when they first enter the care system are often unavoidably driven more by availability than by the much preferred matching of need to resources. However, while the challenges are real, and difficult, even impossible, to overcome, the impact on the child often compounds the trauma she has already experienced.

In most instances, turmoil and instability surround a child coming into care, and the experience of stability which is one of the basic things which she requires is forfeited when she shifts from placement to placement. Thus, her sense of rejection and loss is increased.

Rymaszewska and Philpot (2005), referring to the sense of loss that underpins these children's lives, write:

> As a result of these distortions, children can become aggressive, detached and withdrawn, highly unpredictable in their behavior, and pre-programmed for failure. They can throw temper tantrums, kick, spit and bite. They are frequently self-destructive to the point where they can be suicidal. They may abscond, trash their homes, or steal. They may destroy the very things that are important to them…
>
> They are unable to trust people because it is safer not to do so. They have lost a sense of who they are and, in a literal sense, where they are. They can be driven by an abject terror of having to face the fact that no one wants them. They are, in their own eyes, thrown-away children. This may mean that they take control of their lives by ensuring that others cannot get close to them: they can act to ensure that there is no reason why they should be wanted.

Thus, developmental trauma is a problem far more wide-reaching than the act or acts which caused it, distressing and painful as they may be. Specialised and highly professionalised care is needed if these children are to be helped towards lasting recovery. The toxic stress which they have been subjected to is a process occurring over time in which the experiences of trauma are often multiple in nature, and their effects cumulative and profound. The trauma experience is itself chronic – a damaging experience that cannot be corrected quickly or by any discrete intervention process. What is required is a compensatory experience of healing and recovery in which trust, and the capacity to trust, can be repaired.

There is no basis on which to expect such a recovery process to proceed smoothly. A child who has lived through such adversity will naturally test the boundaries and security of any new situation, sometimes severely so and on multiple occasions. This is an anticipated but nonetheless testing challenge, for the provider, the commissioning authority and not least the child themselves. Stability is key to recovery, and achieving it requires communication, understanding, courage and unwavering commitment. There are no quick fixes or easy solutions, but a clear understanding of the process is required, and a shared, long-term focus on providing a stable, therapeutic, lived experience for the child is the basis on which recovery can be built.

CHAPTER 2

Restorative Parenting

Meeting the Lived Experience of the Child[1]

Instability within often chaotic families is very frequently characteristic of the background of children who come into therapeutic residential care. Coming into the public care system is often seen as an end in itself, as if this move, *per se*, is a form of what the early pioneers of children's charities often called 'rescue'. In fact, reception into care is only the beginning of the process of healing. However, all too often public care does not offer the security, safety and stability which the child needs; indeed, sometimes it can be a place where abuse by others continues.

The life of a child who finds herself in need of a therapeutic environment is overlaid by multiple layers of historic adversity. She will very likely be traumatised through neglect and abuse; and she will be separated from her birth family, but may also have suffered multiple foster care placements, due to breakdown. All this will have had an impact not only on her social self and her psychic and maybe physical health, but will also have had a detrimental effect on her educational attainment. The complexity of these impacts cannot be overstated, or the fact that existing trauma may be compounded by other events which continue in her life.

---

1 The authors acknowledge the paper, 'Introducing Restorative Parenting', by Chris Robinson, Lorraine Aston-Donley and Alicia Brown, on which this chapter, in part, draws.

Thus, the assessment of a child who is to enter a home is an important one. It is a matching process, as much, indeed, as with adoption for some children at the other end of the care spectrum, where they are joining a new family. It is not about filling a vacancy; it is a live process: the age, the needs of the child, the stage of her development, how her presence will impact on the home, and how she will fit in – these are all factors to be borne in mind and which will determine decisions about admission. When the child should be admitted to the home and how that is managed are key considerations.

The therapeutic contract: Establishing time and space for recovery

Fundamentally, restorative parenting involves making a commitment to the child, and we must be confident of being able to fulfil that commitment before agreeing to take a child into the programme. This is a child-centred process, but it is not only about the child and their needs. Looked-after children are engaged with complex systems, within which there may be differing, sometimes conflictual, views about their needs and about where and with whom they should live. Often the courts will have been involved in making major decisions – like who has parental responsibility, who should have contact with a child and who should not. Before making a commitment to a child, there must be a certain level of understanding and acceptance on the part of those asking that we do so, and others significantly involved with the child, that restorative parenting is not a short-term option.

Like any therapeutic intervention, restorative parenting is a process, and part of it involves confronting, experiencing, accepting and overcoming difficult memories and associated emotions. The programme does not demand this, but it is an inevitable part of healing for most children who have suffered trauma and rejection. If a child begins to feel safe enough that she is able to embark upon this process, it is important that the security and support that enabled her to begin to do so remains in place throughout what for many children can be a difficult journey. A premature removal of that security and support can have very damaging consequences. If a child who has suffered trauma and rejection can be carefully helped and encouraged to trust in a therapeutic context – to the point where they begin to express needs and emotions in the developing belief that these will be responded to in a safe and containing way – imagine the hurt and the compounded sense of rejection experienced if that context is then taken away.

The systems which surround looked-after children are in many ways designed to protect them. There are layers upon layers of regulations and requirements within which any provider of therapeutic child care must operate. Regulators rightly demand transparency, the children's rights agenda is very strong, and safeguarding is rightly regarded as a priority. But, within this complex framework of rules and regulations, the child's needs can sometimes be lost within the letter of the law.

Russell: how chronic placement breakdown leads to chaotic behaviour

Russell is 11 years old. He has been in care since he was five. His mother has chronic mental health problems and he was looked after by his grandmother for a time before she returned to her home country of Jamaica. In the six years he has been in care, Russell has had 11 different placements. Eight foster placements failed due to his violent behaviour and tendency to make allegations against carers, teachers and other adults. His previous two residential placements broke down for similar reasons, but his behaviour has also become sexualised, which has added to the difficulty in finding him a suitable home.

Russell has contact with his mother every two weeks. For years, she has consistently told him that he will be returning to live with her as soon as certain obstacles are removed or particular issues are resolved. The obstacles and issues change over time, and the reality is that her circumstances are continually chaotic and her mental health remains poor. Nevertheless, Russell does continue to believe that he is always just weeks away from returning to live with his mother. Because of the history of repeated placement breakdowns and persistent allegations of carer abuse that Russell makes, his case is well known within his home authority and there is senior management overview of his care. Russell speaks to his social worker almost daily, he has an advocate, and he attends all of his review meetings. Encouraged by his mother, Russell contacts ChildLine regularly. He also calls the police at times and he is extremely familiar with all the avenues of complaint open to a child in care.

He is an intelligent child with a keen interest in animals and nature. He can be very kind and caring towards anyone he perceives as being vulnerable or upset in some way, particularly younger children. However, Russell's behaviour is also sometimes volatile and unpredictable. He can be extremely violent towards carers and he sometimes needs to be restrained for his own safety or to protect other people from injury. However, Russell does hurt other people, causing bruises and cuts through punching and kicking. It is not surprising that, in physical struggles with adults, he also sometimes sustains marks and bruises.

If he suffers a bruise during an altercation or restraint, Russell will usually raise a complaint. He will accuse the adults concerned of assault and will involve as many agencies as he is able to in making his complaints. Investigations, interviews, suspensions and strategy meetings follow. Russell will attend any meeting if he is able to and often urges that carers be suspended and prosecuted. For a while, Russell feels he has control, but he, like the system that processes his complaints, is reactive and there is little scope for considering the effects of the long-term process he is engaged in.

Russell is a child with complex problems who must one day be helped to address them. However, the solutions that Russell requires are not to be found within, and he should not be seen as responsible for his reactions, which are, in many ways, an indirect expression of his pain and anger at having been rejected by his mother. To begin to come to terms with this, he must first find stability within a context in which he can relearn trust. Establishing and maintaining that context for him will not be easy, but the time-consuming, extensive negotiations with professionals and the careful navigation of safeguarding processes required is an essential aspect of an effective restorative parenting programme.

Overcoming labels and some relevant theoretical vantage points

Almost all children, even the youngest, who enter the programme, come with a history of placement breakdown. They are often laden with labels like having conduct disorder, oppositional defiant disorder or, very commonly, attention deficit hyperactivity disorder. But look behind those labels and we see that they say nothing about the whole child; they do not show the child as she is, with her strengths, as well as her problems. Needs analysis will reveal a truer picture and show how her problems can be met, rather than just their identification, and whether we can cope with them. Thus, we are not looking at the potentially pejorative descriptions, which are focussed on the child's perceived problems, but at her needs and how these have arisen and been maintained by her experience.

Children who have suffered severe developmental trauma will have attachment problems (see later in the chapter) because their negative experiences will have interfered with their development. Awareness of attachment issues is helpful, not least because it brings an understanding of the child's needs and development as part of their interactive context. Dynamic systems theory teaches an important lesson for those who work therapeutically with children as it acknowledges explicitly the complexity of child development in context (Spencer *et al.*, 2006). Thus, we should not believe that we can easily untangle the complex threads of influence that combine and interact to determine the developmental trajectory and recovery process of an individual child. But dynamic systems theory points, too, to the fact that shaping and modifying the impact and processing of events in context has a critical importance. For restorative parenting this context is *the lived experience of the child*, and thus the approach is an attempt to address all elements that impact upon a child, to provide and promote the optimal contribution to recovery.

The Restorative Parenting recovery programme

The Restorative Parenting recovery programme is founded on therapeutic re-parenting which focuses on addressing the emotional, behavioural, social and developmental needs of the child. It has two stages: the substantive period of up to three years of therapeutic residential care (this period is indicative rather than prescriptive), followed by a transition stage leading to long-term, stable fostering.

Conscious and unconscious have been set at odds by the assumption that the conscious is shallow, visible and easy to reach, while the unconscious is deep, buried and hard to access. And so while everyone can reach the conscious mind, there is a special approach and set of skills needed to deal with the unconscious mind. This is what is often assumed to be 'real' therapy.

However, children grow and develop in the interactive, real world. Thus, for change to be meaningful, it must occur in the world, the reality which the child experiences. It is at this level that restorative parenting operates. The lived experience of the child is the basis for recovery, conscious and unconscious, and the programme does not assume that both cannot be accessed at the same time through the interaction, participation, involvement and achievement that constitute the therapeutic environment – personal, interpersonal and physical. The whole child is the concern of the programme, and it is important to get away from artificial constructs that limit potential. No change is shallow, and no achievement is not meaningful. Real therapy occurs through real experience in the real world.

Restorative parenting involves environmental, interpersonal and individual (that is, care planning for an individual child) approaches. Psychological growth and recovery are facilitated through the practical application of understanding and knowledge taken from a range of relevant research, facilitated through consultation and progress monitoring. Positive behaviour management (see later in the chapter) and a focus on engagement and achievement through active participation in education and a variety of activities appropriate to the particular child are also key elements of the approach.

The education which restorative parenting offers is one from which no child is excluded. Regular consultations and the ready availability of in-house clinical services create an integration of care and clinical practice.

What, then, are the key concepts of restorative parenting and how do they combine to form a comprehensive model of therapeutic child care?

Restorative parenting and other ways of working with children

Macdonald and Millen (2012) undertook a helpful systematic comparison of six therapeutic approaches to residential child care. These were MAP (Model of Attachment Practice), ARC (Attachment, Self-Regulation and Competency), Sanctuary, CARE (Children and Residential Experiences), the resilience model, and social pedagogy. The review showed that common to the approaches were:

- a recognition that children in residential care have suffered trauma and disadvantage

- the belief that staff need to understand the needs and emotions underlying challenging behaviour, rather than simply respond to the behaviour

- a belief that staff and/or children need techniques for being aware of, and regulating their responses to, stressful situations.

With the exception of social pedagogy, all approaches also shared similar underpinnings, particularly in terms of attachment theory (Bowlby, 1969) and recognition of the significance of trauma in the lives of looked-after children. There were different, if overlapping, narratives and frameworks built by the approaches which sought to explain their practice and application. All were concerned, though, with creating nurturing cultures and secure attachment relationships.

In looking at the evidence base for the effectiveness of the approaches, the authors' comparison correctly identified the difficulty in establishing any causal links between the application of a given therapeutic approach to residential care and the outcomes for the children concerned. This is, of course, what dynamic systems theory would predict.

In the beginning

Children who enter the Restorative Parenting programme have suffered developmental trauma; they lack attachment to key figures; and have suffered continuing rejection from their parents. Their experiences have profoundly affected them and they have adapted to cope without the warmth, nurture and love of a consistent and reliable parent. They are in need of a special kind of care and parenting, and the awareness of this actively informs the whole programme of restorative parenting from the very beginning.

Attachment theory

Restorative parenting seeks to re-parent the child. One of the effects of inconsistent, neglectful parenting is that children suffer from disordered attachment. Attachment theory, developed in the 1960s by John Bowlby (1969), proposes that each of us has a blueprint created in the early months of life. Thus, we become attached to an important other (who is usually a parent, often the mother) through a nurturing and loving relationship. If this attachment is secure, we will develop maturely. However, if we suffer rejection, violence, abuse, neglect and lack of bonding, then our mature development is interrupted and may, in extreme circumstances, result in criminal, violent or abusive sexual behaviour. The least damaging effects of insecure attachment will affect adults in their personal and sexual relationships and in their role as parents.

Howe (2000) states that 'attachment behaviour is an instinctive biological drive that propels infants into protective proximity with their main carers whenever they experience anxiety, fear or distress'.

The internal working model is critical here for it is the mechanism through which the child attempts to connect herself, other people and the relationship between them. The quality of the child's caring experiences will determine whether the internal working model is positive or negative.

Beckett (2002) states that:

> a securely attached child...will have a working model of the world in which she herself is worthy of love and attention, others are expected to be responsive and reliable and relationships with others are seen as rewarding and fun.

Children adapt in different ways to their internal working model, and these are:

- secure attachment (the carer is loving and the child is loved)
- ambivalence (the caregiver is inconsistent in how he responds and the child sees herself as dependent and poorly valued)
- avoidant (the caregiver is seen as consistently rejecting and the child is insecure but compulsively self-reliant)
- disorganised (caregivers are seen as frightening or frightened and the child is helpless, or angry and controlling).

(Howe, 2000)

The last response often applies to children who have been maltreated.

While many explanations about the effects of insecure or disordered attachment are psychoanalytical, it is also known that biological damage can result from abuse and violence which interferes with the growth of the brain and that this damage manifests itself externally in various forms of disturbed behaviour (Perry, 1999). We have previously referred (see Chapter 1) to the fact that while this is true about the brain, more is now known about the wider developmental implications and the mechanisms which contribute to such damage.

The human being, and especially the developing child, is complex, and to understand how human beings react to trauma, as well as how they can recover from it, we need to recognise that complexity, and part of that recognition is understanding the intertwining of multiple factors as described in developmental systems theory. However, as we state below, we distinguish between findings about trauma caused by an event – like, for instance, witnessing death, being in an accident – and that caused by neglect and abuse, which is a process and continuous.

What a child learns when nurture fails

Thus, a child whose attachment has been severely disordered or has been made insecure will have deficiencies which have to be compensated for by re-parenting within a therapeutic regime which is containing and accepting. The children who come into the Restorative Parenting programme have learned not to express needs because they do not expect that they will be met. As Robinson *et al.* (undated) explain:

> At a basic level, this can be about food, the need for warmth and basic comforts. Some children would rather steal food than be given it, they would rather sleep on the floor than in a bed and will reject, sometimes angrily or violently, any offer of comfort or support.

Through the experience of disordered or disrupted attachments the child fails to develop an internal consistency of response. This is one of attachment theory's key lessons (Bowlby, 1969). She has no expectation of being listened to or understood by adults.

The child who faces chronic unpredictability, who does not know what an adult's reaction will be to her own behaviour, lives with chronic stress, described as 'toxic stress'. This can, for example, be about food (what it will be like; whether it is adequate; or when it will come or even whether it will come at all) or warmth (sometimes the home is freezing, sometimes too hot, sometimes it is okay). A child who cries may be picked up and cuddled, left to cry or be hit – all reactions may come from the same adult at different times. A child wanting to sleep may be allowed to sleep or not allowed to sleep; or may be woken from sleep. Treated in this way a child may respond in different ways at different times – she may respond positively or negatively, or not at all. The child's internal world becomes confused and her own responses unpredictable.

The child may also display elements of learned helplessness (Seligman, 1972), whereby she disengages and learns not to escape adverse experiences, even if she is able to do so or an escape route is presented.

Van der Kolk (2014) illustrates the idea of learned helplessness by graphically describing the experiments of Maier and Seligman (1976), whereby they had repeatedly administered painful electric shocks to dogs trapped in locked cages. They called this 'inescapable shock' because, after administering several courses of shock, the cage doors were opened and the dogs were then shocked again. A control group of dogs had never been shocked and immediately ran away, but those shocked earlier made no attempt to escape, even when the door was wide open; 'they just lay there, whimpering and defecating'.

Van der Kolk concludes from this:

> Scared animals return home, regardless of whether home is safe or frightening. I thought about my patients with abusive families who kept going back to be hurt again. Are traumatised people condemned to seek refuge in what is familiar? If so, why, and is it possible to help them become attached to places and activities which are safe and pleasurable?

Unless this is fully understood on the part of those working with the child and they embed it in their practice, they can too easily attribute to the child a conscious motivation that can make them appear confusing, rejecting, aggressive, avoidant or overly compliant. (See the section on page 33, 'Making helpful attributions'.)

More commonly, children who have experienced chronically unreliable, inconsistent parenting engage in extreme behaviour, and create stress, mayhem and conflict around them. They want to stay at a distance because it is only at an emotional distance that they are able to manage interactions with adults. Because of their experience, they cannot trust or emotionally engage with adults in a healthy way.

Robinson *et al.* (undated), drawing on Lamb (2005) and Lewis (2005), go on to state that:

> restorative parenting demands exceptional levels of acceptance and consistency from the therapeutic parents who care for the children. The adults who care for a child, and to some extent the other children in the home, become the key social network within which there must be as many opportunities as possible for the child to reliably experience the consistent and responsive care which they have been previously lacking. This social network is the context in which the child can safely experience attachments of different intensities and forms with different people.

The impact of trauma

It is a core principle, recognised by restorative parenting, that trauma results for children who have been subject to abuse, neglect and parental rejection. But the nature and extent of the trauma is not discrete or fixed in time and place. As we have seen, the language commonly used to discuss trauma is adapted from the literature on post-traumatic stress disorder (PTSD). This may not be accurate or appropriate, as it fails to capture the pervasive nature of the repetitive and often chronic stress experienced by the children with whom we are concerned here. Most of these children have suffered chronic adversity, rejection and abuse over many years. Thus, this trauma is often a process and not an event, which cannot be reduced to discrete episodes (van der Kolk, 2003).

We are learning through contemporary research to move away from narrow models of neurology which link childhood trauma to discrete changes in brain anatomy. Above we have referred to toxic childhood stress, which impacts on developing biological systems in diffuse and enduring ways. This is what the results of the chronic trauma of child abuse, neglect and parental rejection are increasingly recognised as (Evans and Kim, 2012).

The responses of a child to environmental and social stressors are significantly determined by their predictive adaptive response (PAR), as we have seen. The concept of PAR derives from evolutionary biology and has been subject to research into physical health conditions and the development of disease processes. It is analogous to an embedded weather forecast which programmes someone's expectations of living conditions during early life. When children have been exposed to toxic childhood stress, their reactions to subsequent stress stimuli become programmed to start quicker, to last longer and to be of greater intensity (Carroll *et al.*, 2013). Consequently, these children have a substantially reduced ability to regulate their physiological, emotional and behavioural responding.

Multi-sensory sensitivities result from toxic childhood stress and there are thus changes to the PAR, which interact to cause difficulties for the child in re-calibrating arousal levels and experiencing hypersensitivity to the general environment (van der Kolk, 2003).

The therapeutic environment, staff and consultations

A child who has been traumatised reacts differently to stimuli which other children would not notice or might even positively relish – like bright or garish colours. Thus, a therapeutic environment, must be a calming and consistent one, with a low stimulus, which encourages a feeling of belonging, warmth and homeliness. How this is created we discuss in detail in Chapter 3.

Staff work as a team within the therapeutic environment, and a team needs to work together and to engage in consultation, where its members are consulted. This we discuss more fully in Chapter 8.

Making helpful attributions

Children who have been abused have not only been treated negatively, sexually and physically, but also in the way that adults have reacted to them intellectually and emotionally. They may never have been told that they are good or doing well or have achieved something, their strengths have never been consistently recognised, their talents lie dormant for want of encouragement and their interests receive no stimulus.

Any child, even if not sexually or physically abused, would develop a poor self-perception and negative view of themselves when treated in this way. For those who have been abused, such treatment only compounds and makes worse their condition. Thus, it is essential that this narrative is broken and replaced by a new one which will help to re-make the child's perception of herself. This means an emphasis on coping and strength – what the child can do and is capable of – which can often foster previously obscured and unrecognised and unacknowledged strengths and skills.

Each child is unique; each process that seeks to change her narrative is peculiar to her. It is also a continual process because recovery is not a straight, foreseeable and predictable trajectory. Recovery not only involves times of slipping back but itself throws up new challenges of behavioural and emotional expression that were not foreseen when the process began. However, this must be understood and interpreted as being part of the recovery process rather than as failures to learn or understand, which can easily happen if a problem-focussed mindset is allowed to develop.

Perspective is difficult to maintain without the right kind of support. Consultation, supervision, training and continuing education are vital elements of restorative parenting.

Consultation

All the therapeutic parenting teams meet monthly with a member of the clinical team, normally a practitioner psychologist. The consultation is organised along solution-orientated lines, with a focus on helping the child to participate positively in social activities, in building relationships and sharing, in education and in developing their own interests and talents. Markers of progress are the building blocks which contribute to success in these areas (see the Appendix) and, through the process of consultation, matters such as helping the child to improve their self-care skills and to overcome barriers to participation and achievement are routinely addressed.

The solution focus of consultation does not mean that problems are not discussed, but rather than dwell on how difficult or limiting these appear, the question is about how the difficulties are managed successfully, how they can be reduced and what is needed to help the child to progress. The process of consultation helps to bring direction to the team by creating and maintaining a shared understanding of how everyone is helping the child to recover. The psychologist who leads the consultation does not take the role of expert and the process is collaborative, as it is only through sharing ownership of the responsibility and key parenting tasks that they can be effectively delivered.

Seeing the child in a positive light

No child is so utterly damaged that she does not very occasionally, and probably briefly, show some instinctive pleasure from engagement and success, even when she seems to have withdrawn from almost any form of emotional interaction. The focus on problems looks at what the child lacks, what she cannot do. We need to look at what she can do, what her competencies are, and then to bring those competencies across contexts.

For example, a girl is said to lack the ability to concentrate but can spend, literally, hours playing a highly complex computer game. To do this she will be exercising lateral thinking, concentration, memory, mental rehearsal, pride in achievement, motivation, competitiveness and problem solving. Who is to say that such competencies cannot be practised in other areas? Likewise, there is the boy who creates his own room, chooses the furniture and decoration, and yet every so often destroys it. But in creating the room he has shown judgement, discernment, taste, an eye for design and colour, and the placing of objects and furniture. He has done this through concentration and application.

The contexts for both these children are potentially as wide, as they are able to exploit their competencies. And when a child comes up against a problem in one context, she has the memory of success in another context to indicate that the new problem is not insoluble.

What has made such rare occasions possible? Why has the child reacted in this positive way? Taking note of such occasions, as restorative parenting does, is a way of exploring what made them possible for a child. These are small islands of success where clues lie buried about a child's strengths and attributes, which can be excavated so that they can be built upon in the future. A key to promoting positive progress is developing what Seligman (2002) describes as a child's signature strengths – all children have some talent, and identifying them is a key for staff.

A therapeutic parent may make a range of attributions in response to a child's challenging behaviour. Unhelpfully, they may make personal, internal attributions of the child not liking them and acting out of a sense of malice: 'She doesn't like me and is deliberately trying to upset me.' More constructively, the therapeutic parent may attribute the child's behaviour to external drivers – seeing it as a result of emotional pain. Attributions influence perceptions and interpretations – a personal/internal attribution in relation to a child's behaviour will make it much more difficult to recognise strengths and can lead to any positive effort the child makes being dismissed as false or deliberately misleading: 'He can pretend to be good.' External attributions allow the child and her strengths and skills to be seen positively and encouraged as keys, which can open up her talents.

The child and the adult are at the centre

Care and attention to environments, expert consultation or treating a child positively – all these are necessary. But at the core of care is the relationship between children and their therapeutic parents (see Chapter 4).

The interaction between child and adult is a point of learning to which restorative parenting returns time and again; it is here that recovery is helped or undone and is a key point of learning. The child must know consistently from the adult that acceptance and trust are genuinely and reliably available. We have said before that their history means that traumatised children have no expectation that their needs will be reliably met, and they are just as likely to react negatively to success and positive interactions as they are setbacks and rejection. However, the positive, responsive and accepting adult has to remain consistently available.

The positive way to manage behaviour

The positive behaviour support model is internationally recognised and comparatively modern. It stems from the United States of America, where it was developed for use with adults with learning disabilities, but has been adopted increasingly for use in schools as an alternative to aversive, problem-focussed systems of behaviour management.

Based on principles of applied behaviour analysis, it is used by restorative parenting to manage challenging behaviour by children. The Restorative Parenting programme makes use of a basic understanding that behaviour serves a purpose and is influenced by the environment, both physical and social, which, therefore, has to be considered. The programme, using the model, therefore focuses on helping children to learn new skills better to communicate their needs in more socially acceptable and empowering ways. When a child exhibits challenging behaviour, it is always a way of conveying some underlying need, anxiety or fear. This must, of course, be recognised in the positive attributions, to which we have referred to above, made by the adults caring for them.

These behaviours help us to see how the child can be taught alternative skills, which will not only empower her to exert more control over her life but also help reduce her self-limiting behaviours. The place of sanctions and rewards within positive behaviour management is valid only insofar as they assist the child to learn new behaviours. Understanding, guiding and modelling are more prominent features within the programme.

Practical principles which guide the positive behaviour model are listed below:

- Rather than attempt to control someone's behaviour, support them in the process of changing it.

- Challenging behaviour masks a need, often unmet, and so the behaviour is telling us something.

- Everyone possesses strengths and attributes which can be realised.

- Compassion and respect for a person trump any attitude toward behaviour.

- Responding positively is more productive and effective than being coercive or punishing.

The model looks at strategies and ways to help the child reduce challenging behaviour and increase her quality of life through teaching her new skills and adjusting her environment to promote positive behaviour changes.

If successful, both the child's success and personal satisfaction and her social interactions in school, home and community will have increased.

To practise the model you need to identify and understand the behaviour, to see what the child is 'telling' you. You also have to improve the child's quality of life to reduce her challenging behaviour and assist her in changing her behaviour.

You should also make changes to environments, to routines and to expectations in order to reduce or remove triggers and prevent behavioural issues developing. Agree intervention strategies for each child with the aim of de-escalating situations at an early point and avoiding problems developing into potential crisis points. The strategies that are effective may vary from child to child within the overall positive behaviour management framework, and each child should have their own behaviour support plan.

Staff should model positive behaviour; they should teach new ways whereby a child can communicate her needs; and develop positive interventions when challenging behaviour is exhibited. Staff should also continue to evaluate the support strategies used. In this the whole staff team (and, where there is contact, the family, too) needs to be involved. The organisation has to offer support to staff undertaking this work.

It is essential for all adults, whether or not they have direct contact with children – thus, for example, staff working in human relations and office staff – to receive training in positive behaviour management. This is because the way different parts of an organisation have an impact on each other is the way that the whole organisation works. That completed, the main focus should be to have a clear understanding of what challenging behaviours are, why the children present specific behaviours, what preventative measures can be implemented to make changes to the child's environment and how to teach the child to develop new skills to manage their own behaviours. This can only be achieved through high levels of consistency.

Individual therapy and life story work

Individual therapy can be arranged for children, but is not usually provided as a long-term adjunct to the security and stability delivered through the overall programme. All children are treated individually through their relationship with their key worker, and more formal therapy, if required, is provided by members of the clinical team or from accredited professionals contracted for the purpose. While not a routine aspect of the therapeutic programme, individual therapy can be used when there are particular issues that may be restricting a child's progress.

The role of individual therapy

The majority of children referred to the Restorative Parenting programme have a history of previous involvement with local Child and Adolescent Mental Health Services. Many of them have received extensive individual input in an attempt to help them better manage and cope with sometimes extreme emotions and behaviours. Fundamentally, these emotions and behaviours stem from a breakdown of trust and the profound sense of rejection that results from family breakdown. It follows that the child is most in need of nurture and re-parenting that will allow her to regain trust in carers so that she can express her needs, thoughts and feelings, safe in the knowledge that she will not be faced with further rejection. This process inevitably involves extensive testing of trust and boundaries, through many different means, and the reliability and consistency of nurturing, of people and of safe contexts, are a key part of what restorative parenting gives to the child.

The progress of all children placed in the Restorative Parenting recovery programme is continually monitored and formally evaluated on a monthly basis.

Individual therapy is available to all children placed on the programme if required, but it is neither necessary nor helpful for all children to be routinely given such input. Clinically supervised key work sessions can address many issues limiting progress in a helpful way, without impacting upon a child's experience through adding on the requirement of formal therapy sessions. Restorative parenting aims to engage the child in education, activities and social experiences which build trust and emotional resilience. There are situations where individual therapy can act as a barrier to such engagement, and the benefits or otherwise of any such provision are assessed against measures of overall progress.

In general, if a child is progressing through participation in the overall recovery programme, it is not expected that they will be given individual therapy sessions. Input from our psychologists and other members of the clinical team will be indirect, through targeted consultation, supervision and general oversight of the child's progress.

If monitoring and evaluation indicate that a child is not making expected levels of progress, individual therapeutic input is one of a range of options which are considered.

The programme is concerned with providing a therapeutic lived experience, and it is the immersion of the child within that lived experience which is the key vehicle of change and therapeutic growth. Individual therapy can sometimes be useful insofar as it can address and remove barriers to the child positively accessing that experience, but it's important to consider other factors, both internal and external to the programme, which might also be limiting progress. If these can be helpfully modified or removed, one should remove them first, recognising that the children we look after are more than averagely vulnerable to stress. Sometimes arranging individual therapy for a child is far easier than addressing problems elsewhere in the system, such as unreliable contact arrangements. But the underlying assumption that, through individual therapy, the child can or should be helped to cope with situations or circumstances that are highly stressful to them is not something that should be accepted, unless those situations or circumstances are themselves entirely unavoidable.

In those circumstances where individual therapy is considered helpful, it is generally provided by the in-house clinical teams who have skills and experience in systemic, solution-focussed, cognitive behavioural and more exploratory therapeutic approaches. Occasionally, a child will have an identified therapeutic need which is not available within the programme, such as long-term psychodynamic work. In this case, we make use of qualified and registered practitioners from the independent sector who provide regular updates on progress and are encouraged to attend review meetings as key professionals working with the child.

Life story work

As we achieve increasing stability within the therapeutic placement, it becomes necessary to help a child understand why she came into care and what the future will hold for her. Too often a child coming into care, shorn of so much that is familiar, may receive only limited information or explanations as to why she may have been removed from her home, or at best this information may be disjointed and full of inconsistencies. Life story work communicates the child's story in a manner which is helpful to the child and her carers.

With the Restorative Parenting programme, it is children who are approaching the final stages of recovery who will undertake life story work. It is at the latter stage in the programme that the children have both the personal resilience and the long-term security of context to find the most therapeutic value in life story work.

Life story work with children means working with a child to amass the evidence of her life, to tell her story, to select materials that illustrate that story, and to write, or help the child to write, the story herself (Rose and Philpot, 2004).

It allows the child to explore her place in the world, through an explanation of her past and the context in which it has been lived. It is embarked on between 12 and 18 months after the child has entered the home.

It is an approach that seeks not only to answer the questions of what, why and when about the child's life, but also who. Who helped the child or who harmed her? In short, how did I get where I am? Connor *et al.* (1985) write about life story work and adoption, but they rightly say that it is about 'unravelling confusion and discarding some of the negative emotional baggage which the child has carried for so long'.

Life story work is, then, about the identity of the child, and not only how the past has shaped that identity but what that past is. Uncovering that past is part of the therapeutic process, and so more than the merely chronological or even factual. As Rose and Philpot (2004) say: 'Life story work is about the people in the child's life, what happened to the child and the reasons why those things happened. It is not, and cannot be, a simple narrative or description.'

As part of this you or the child may have to interview people from the child's past, from foster parents to parents, and from social workers to teachers and residential workers. Social work and court reports have to be read; official documents like birth, marriage and death certificates found; and electoral registers searched. There may be visits (sometimes with the child) to places where she has lived or which are significant to her. It may be necessary to talk with the child at some length and liaise with her foster parent or carer and others currently working with her. All this will result in a life story book.

None of us can ignore our past, and this applies even more to traumatised children, because for them to try to move on would be impossible if the past were ever-present.

From problem to possibility

It is both a challenge and an opportunity to recognise, as we noted above, that childhood trauma is complex and occurs in the dynamic context of growth and development and the interdependence of action and experience. Recognising this complexity and the processes that go with it, restorative parenting does not seek to provide a therapeutic response to the chronic impact of toxic childhood stress in a separate, unintegrated way. The essence of the programme is that it is multi-dimensional, with a focus on the lived experience of the child, which makes it holistic.

Robinson *et al.* (undated) state:

> Restorative parenting is informed by knowledge of child development and parenting needs. It is informed by dynamic systems theory, attachment theory, attribution theory, positive psychology and research into the encoding, processing and impacts of traumatic experience. Our practice is guided by knowledge and experience of the power of narrative and reframing, solution focused approaches and the insights provided by the Pillars of Parenting. The context created by Restorative Parenting is responsive, consistent and attuned to children's needs. It provides the space – environmental and interpersonal – within which recovery can take place. At a basic level this translates into four key elements:
>
> - the right people
> - the right environment
> - translate learning into practice
> - monitor progress.

The environment and the characteristics of people who are best suited to providing restorative parenting are discussed in detail in other chapters. The role of training, support and consultation in ensuring that the theory of restorative parenting is translated into practice is discussed in Chapter 8. In order to monitor progress through the programme, we use the Restorative Parenting Recovery Index (see the Appendix).

However, before discussing the index, we need to explain that underpinning the index there are five elements which cover a child's needs for security, warmth and relationships as a basis for emotional growth and developing resilience. They are:

- self-care

- forming relationships and attachments

- self-perception

- self-management and self-awareness

- emotional competence.

The completion of the index means that every month a child's progress is checked against each of the five elements, each of which involves answering structured questions about the child, to ensure that the child's progress is being achieved. The index is completed by recording observations of the child's presentation and behaviour in different settings and her reactions and responses to different situations and challenges. The index also helps one to identify any problem areas for that month. These areas of concern can then be discussed during consultations and made into priority parenting tasks for the following month.

Restorative parenting at a glance

Figure 2.1 shows a visual representation of restorative parenting. At the most basic level it refers to the environmental aspects of homes. A child can start to grow emotionally and psychologically once these aspects are in place and the environment is stable and secure. Investment in extracurricular activities focussing on a child's signature strengths can help build resilience and social connectedness. As the child becomes more confident and develops improved self-management, an appropriate school can be found and, finally, a stable long-term foster placement.

Psychological growth and resilience	Re-integration	Environment
• Consultations, reflection, goal setting • Individual work including relationship building • Activities – engagement, achievements, signature strengths • Group – social connectedness • Family	• Society • School • Family	• Physical • Interpersonal • Personal

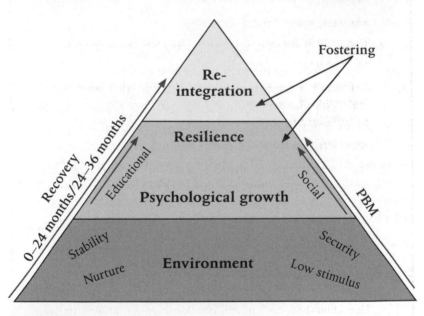

Figure 2.1: The Restorative Parenting picture

Restorative Parenting is an integrated programme that meets traumatised children where they are; that seeks, through a therapeutic environment, therapeutic parenting and foster care, to restore what they have lost or never had – a positive experience of parenting, which will heal the wounds they have suffered and equip them to be healthy adults and useful citizens and good parents. It does so by finding what is good, useful and positive in the child, to recognise and make use of their innate skills and abilities, which have been unrecognised, unacknowledged or played down. In doing this restorative parenting regards the child as a whole person.

Sarah, who never knew where she stood with her parents

Sarah had two parents who were alcoholics. She would return from school and sometimes go straight to bed and not be asked about her day. At other times her parents would be affectionate, hug her and talk to her about school. On another day she could be violently assaulted. Thus, she would come home not knowing what to expect. In response she learned to be inexpressive and not to speak and to have no emotional engagement at all. Her parents' actions, which were based on their state of intoxication, resulted in a child who became distant, remote and emotionally detached.

All children coming to a residential home require reassurance, and Sarah particularly so. Thus, two therapeutic parents worked with her as joint key workers to ensure that one person was always available to her. It was they who gave her the consistency that she lacked, which might be a reassuring greeting like, 'Hello, good to see you again' when she came back from somewhere, or to make sure that one of them was there when she went to school and when she returned each day. But this is a process that happens in small steps, and every so often Sarah would challenge the trust and reliability. Only over a longer period of time did such consistency and reassurance allow her to trust that adults could be reliable.

CHAPTER 3

A Home for the Child

Creating a Therapeutic Environment

Much of the literature about children's residential care concentrates on what happens within the home – how children and staff interact; how challenging behaviour is met; the rules that govern day-to-day life; staff management, and so on. All of this is, of course, relevant, and much is still open to question as to how effective regimes are. How children react, however, is often determined by factors other than their relationships with other children and staff in the home; indeed those relationships and more can be influenced *by* the physical environment.

That said, while it is axiomatic that a home – and we use the word 'home' rather than the more institutional 'house' – should be welcoming, warm, friendly and as near as possible an approximation to what an ordinary home should be, that itself is not enough if the children living there have suffered abuse and trauma.

How a home is designed and decorated requires fine attention to detail, with the needs of the children who are to live there being the most central consideration. This means that the physical environment must be specifically designed to meet the needs of the children if it is to be the context in which therapeutic parenting takes place. It is a *total* environment that, in a way, can be said to complement the emotional availability and commitment of the therapeutic parent to the child. And so *every* part of a child's life, their lived experience, is seen as offering an opportunity with the environment and the setting for parenting. The physical environment in which children live can be, in many ways, as important as the emotional one and the relationships they share. The home in which the child lives should offer therapeutic opportunities, ones both emotionally and physically significant. As all aspects of a child's life can be seen to have therapeutic potential, so the home – the therapeutic environment – is thoughtfully designed as a context in which to realise that potential.

How a child should see her home

A child who has been neglected or abused will often also have known an unstable, even chaotic lifestyle, and the physical environment from which she will have come will often have unpleasant associations, as well as being unpleasant *per se*. The general standard of care may well have been poor, with the child lacking in stimulation and the security of a dependable routine, as well as being materially deprived of the comforts of a more nurturing home.

For some such children the residential home to which they come may be the first proper home they have experienced; or some may have been in unsatisfactory (given their needs) mainstream residential accommodation. They will not have regarded this as home in any meaningful sense if it, too, lacked a sense of security and stability in which they could first feel safe before beginning to trust. Indeed, if, for example, the other young people there were absconding, or being disruptive or abusive, and if there was a lack of communication and understanding, the child may have been further traumatised.

Many younger children will have probably gone into foster care, when taken into care, and the instability of the family home can then too often have been replicated, with multiple placements and foster carers and social workers going in and out of their lives. The new, therapeutic home to which they have now come must be one that offers them safety, security, rootedness and a sense of belonging, and sets a standard for what to expect of one's home.

By definition, most of these children will have suffered a breakdown in consistent parenting and nurturing, and some may have suffered physical and sexual abuse, neglect, abandonment or parental problems like alcohol misuse and drugs. Indeed, some will have no consistent experience of being looked after by an adult at all.

Initially, they can easily resist the therapeutic parent's attempt to look after them, to offer them care – why shouldn't they? Trust in adults is not something that they are used to. However, the child comes not only to a home that is warm, friendly and safe but one which is taken care of by the therapeutic parent: that staff member sees that things are put back or mended or replaced; or brings a toy to the child in her room which has been left elsewhere. Such care for the home, which, importantly, is the *child's* home, is visibly demonstrating to the child that the therapeutic parent is available and determined to offer personal care and commitment to her.

It is important that the therapeutic parent's role goes beyond the specific tasks of caring for and supporting the child; it is about looking after a home where the child is now living. The expectation must be that maintaining standards in the home is everyone's task, not just one allocated to key workers or those in senior positions.

What do we need to remember when designing and decorating the home? This is important to consider because children react to trauma in different ways and they express their pain differently. Each child experiences different triggers, some of which are environmental and can evoke memories and, often, as a result, stress or disruptive behaviour, sometimes behaviour injurious to themselves alone, but sometimes also to others.

Thus, noise, colour and brightness affect children differently, but all rooms need to be neutral in colour, without glaring lights. (See 'Carole in the light' later in the chapter.) Floors should be carpeted and not made of wood so that they do not echo. Temperatures in the home need to be kept neither hot nor cold. The colours of furniture need to be uniform. A playroom will be colourful, with toys and posters, but, again, garish colours are to be avoided. While the creation of such an environment aims, in part, to avoid high, expressed emotion, that does not mean, of course, that children cannot express themselves and should be encouraged to do so.

Encoding – the turning of information into memories – happens at a rapid rate during a traumatic incident, at an aural, auditory and cognitive level, as the senses take in experiences rather as a rapidly set camera films a sports event. Thus, aspects of the environment can subsequently trigger these buried 'recordings' through the child's sensory sensitivities.

While children can choose their own room colours, décor, furniture and decorations to suit their tastes and interests, they will naturally tend to avoid anything which is aversive. The child knows what she finds aversive, but where adults are responsible for how a space which is shared by all looks and feels, they need to learn.

A therapeutic children's home needs to be considered from a sensory perspective, the aim being to help achieve an optimum background environment by removing those features which, while unplanned and often unnoticed, nevertheless can have a significant sensory impact.

It is neither necessary nor useful to create 'clinical' spaces free of colour or of light and furnishings that have a homely feel. A children's home should be a place of nurture, and there is a balance to be made between sensory neutrality and an environment which has a warm and welcoming feel. In our experience, this has not been too difficult to achieve. The homes do not look or feel sterile, but the air of relaxation they have is consciously achieved and monitored.

Even before a baby is born parents plan ahead. They think about the baby's first clothes and toys and the room and its decoration. Children who come into care deserve just as much thought and planning, as to the environment they will enter, as the soon-to-be-born baby. Too often, though, public care is institutionalised and impersonal, with little evidence of the personal or of individual investment.

So, before a child moves into a home, she should be encouraged to bring something (most commonly a toy) to leave in what will be her room. In turn, the home gives her something (a pen, a toy, a diary, a book, something which interests the child). It is an exchange – something important from where the child has been to and from the place where she will live.

The symbolism of the left or received item has longer-term implications. Once a child is living in the home with all her possessions, then the fact that she can feel that they can be left, and that they will not disappear or be damaged, helps that child to feel even more a sense that she belongs to the community, that the home is *her* home – all the home, not just that she and her possessions are secure and safe only in their own room.

Cairns (2002) could be referring to the role of the therapeutic parent in the home when she writes:

All those who have made a commitment to the child now have to work together to construct an environment which will enable the child to move together from the cold and lonely wasteland of unmet attachment needs to the warmth and safety and supportiveness of secure attachment relationships...

It will be an environment in which those close to the child are adopting a consistent approach which meets the child's needs, adapting the approach to fit their own role with the child but proving great consistency in the structures surrounding the child.

The personal touch

The therapeutic parent, as we will show (Chapter 4), consistently compensates the child with positive experiences for the deficiencies in nurture she has met at the hands of her parents. This requires consistent focus and effort and attention to the total environment. This runs from care to personal interactions; from meal times to bedtimes; and all that goes on in between and around.

It is important to find out, too, what a child's interests are before she arrives at the home. For example, the boy who was a Chelsea fan had his room decorated in the team's colours, with team-themed bed linen in time for his arrival. This allowed him immediately to feel that this was 'his' room. It is also a way of signifying to him that he is worth the thought and attention to detail, that he is welcomed and wanted.

A bedroom should be a place of comfort, safety and sanctuary, but for some children it may be one of unhappy, even terrifying, memories. So a bedroom allotted to a child is important in all kinds of ways. Importantly, in contrast to where she has lived before, which may have been the site of abuse and lack of privacy, this bedroom is the child's own; it is not only one where, as we have said, she has chosen the décor, and one free of the triggers that can provoke unwanted memories, but it is a private space, somewhere where others ask permission to enter; and can express the child's personality even before she has moved in.

But a pleasant bedroom is not enough. Bedtime for a child who has been abused may be a time of anxiety. For this child a bed may be something about which they feel at the very least ambivalent. Sleep may be a prelude to nightmares.

In the day, in the light, there are people and objects that give comfort. In the dark, on one's own, they are not there to hold onto. Being in a room on one's own – in fact, the very act of going to sleep – requires the child to be trusting. A comfort blanket, a favoured toy, a night-time story, a glass of milk – all of these are part of a therapeutic environment that can be a help at a time like this. In the light the room is pleasant; at night that can't be seen, so a soft, dim light, in the room or outside, may be comforting. It is also important that the house should be quiet (and likewise the area outside).

Daws (1993) writes with regard to a baby's going to bed, which applies equally to older children:

> Sleeping problems illustrate difficulties at every stage. Receptivity to the needs of a baby, sensitivity to their fears and spontaneous offering of comfort need to be tempered with a gradual setting of limits. Understanding of a baby's fears enables a parent to contain those fears; the baby gradually learns to manage them himself.

However, waking and getting up may be as problematic for a child who has been abused as going to bed. The day ahead, after all, is not something that a child's experience suggests will be pleasant, and it could be painful.

A child should always be woken by their therapeutic parent, with whom they have a significant relationship. When this cannot be done, then someone new to the home should not wake the child; that needs to be someone with whom the child is, at the very least, familiar. (A chair should always be in the room which the therapeutic parent can use, as the child may not like the adult sitting on the bed.)

And how does the child like to be woken – when she is still asleep; when dozing; with a glass of milk; by a tap on the door; a gentle shake; by the curtains being opened? Any of these may suit a different child.

Once the child is up and ready to leave the room, she needs to find a warm and welcoming house, where others are preparing for the day to come. This is a signifier of the positive day ahead.

The child will be coming down to breakfast, and here is a way that a home can also provide a sense of belonging that assists the child's developing sense of identity and worth. This is because one of the most important ways that these qualities can be engendered is the way in which meal times are organised. In all societies and cultures, meals are a means by which friends and family come together, often just to be with one another, sometimes to celebrate an event particular to them – a home coming or a leave taking – or a shared event, like a birthday. And so, in the home, there are shared meal times, when everyone sits down together. It is important, then, that there are sufficient spaces for all children to sit down together, otherwise sitting separately could, later on, be perceived by the child as rejection.

Children can decide what to eat; some take part in food preparation and cooking (learning by watching rather than specific instruction); they take part in shopping; and some are involved in budgeting.

There will be, though, other children, not yet ready to participate with others, who will act differently – they will sit at the table but seek to dominate by shouting or kicking other children under the table (see 'Tommy, the boy with potatoes in his pockets' later in the chapter). Some children may not know how to share, and the whole experience of sitting down at a table to eat may be unfamiliar to them.

A word on language

We have said how look and touch and degrees of light and colour are important. But too often residential care is made institutional by the language used by staff, and also the use to which staff put the building.

So, for example, how we talk about things influences how we do them, even though for many staff institutional language can give some kind of assurance. Staff meetings should not be held in homes, with the exception of LAC reviews with the reviewing officer, where regulatory requirement demands that offices have to be sited in homes for access to records, logs and the like, and, of course, fire exit signs have to be in place and certain notices. Homes, as we have said, are just that, and not 'houses'. There are no 'unit cars', only cars; while words like 'shift' and 'rota' should be avoided, and first names are used for staff, who to the children are not called 'staff'.

This sense of belonging is also encouraged by children's school paintings and photographs being kept safely in the house, where they can be discussed with the therapeutic parent and talked about during contact with parents.

The principle about a home is emphasised by Pughe and Philpot (2007), and will determine so much else:

> A home where children live should reflect their personalities as much as those of their parents. Within a residential home this is even more important. The carers who work there may sleep in, but it is not their home; *it is, however, home to the children.* (Our italics)

Remember, too, that many children have led lives of terrible deprivation, both physically (in terms of possessions and general health) and emotionally. What they have been given – a toy, say – may have been from an abuser wanting to reassure them or groom them. Their new home, then, should be one where games, toys, books, comics and the like are plentiful and offer choice. Playing, too, can offer them the chance to make relationships, based on fun, with the other children and therapeutic parents.

When children live in an environment which is accepting, loving, warm and aesthetically pleasing they internalise how those who care for them feel about them, that they are entitled to the best and are valued.

Inside and outside

The outside of a home is also important, not least what its appearance expresses to those who live there and those who are neighbours. It is important that homes should not be in inner cities or in high crime areas but rather in quiet neighbourhoods. They should be detached properties, with a garden, where boundaries are important, so they should have fences or hedges, but should be indistinguishable from neighbouring properties. This will mean, for example, that they do not have car parks, and staff should be encouraged not all to park outside so that there are no more than one or two cars there at any one time. As with boundaries in relationships, physical boundaries should be well maintained and respected; and gates should be ones that one would expect for properties of a similar kind, not cheap or standard ones.

As the inside of the home is well cared for, so should gardens and the front of homes. Hedges should be trimmed and lawns cut and flowers tended, but not such that children feel intimidated about using the garden and playing there; they should feel that this, too, is 'theirs'. Such care is, again, saying something to the child about the value which is placed on her.

If a school is adjacent to the home, make sure that it cannot be reached by connecting doors.

The life of the home

Henry Maier's work in the 1980s addressed the spatial design elements of care environments for children and how these interacted with and shaped the social living experience. Maier also spoke of the 'rhythms of care' and 'the importance of consistency and dependability, in terms of interactions and environment' (Maier, 1981). These elements are particularly important when one considers that, as discussed earlier, many children come into residential homes from abusive chaotic homes, where predictability of any sort may have been absent.

An important part of the therapeutic environment is routine for children, for whom a sense of routine may be completely alien and whose waking, sleeping and eating may have been arbitrary and certainly out of their control. But here routine does not imply rules or set systems, because this is about authorative, not authoritarian, parenting. Within the Restorative Parenting programme, routine symbolises reliability, consistency and predictability, which contribute to a safe and secure environment.

We have mentioned the place of meal times in this. But also children will be up by a certain time, their beds made, they will breakfast together at a set time and then be off to school. When they come home, they may engage in different activities – watching

TV, reading or being read to, going to the cinema or club of some kind – but differing activities does not mean lack of routine. All this may sound practical, but much of it requires the therapeutic parent to work with or help the child – making a bed or reading a story – and that shows the child, too, that the therapeutic parent is giving of himself.

Before the children go to bed, there may be tidying up to be done and preparations for the next day. These are often practical tasks, and practical tasks to be successfully carried out involve routine and consistency.

Meal times – breakfast, lunch and dinner – are important not only for the reasons already stated: the sense of belonging and community which they engender as everyone sits together and enjoys the meal and the company of others. But preparation – which includes the laying of the table – is important, as is the clearing away and washing up. All children can play some part in this, no matter how much or how little their age and abilities allows them to do so. And in doing that they learn – at a very practical level this may be learning to cook – to co-operate and share. This communal coming together also shows a concern for others – we are all helping one another to get the meal ready and to deal with what we have to do after we have eaten. And, of course, in doing this, children observe what the therapeutic parents are doing, which is for them and so an encouragement that they, too, take part; indeed, here, as elsewhere, the therapeutic parent is a very obvious role model.

Pets

While a home should be as much like an ordinary home, living within an ordinary family as possible, such homes and families do tend to have pets, but the keeping of pets is inadvisable for children who may well have difficulty looking after themselves. The children may well have difficulty in regulating their emotions and can be subject to strong impulses and sometimes violent behaviours over which they have little control.

Caring for a pet can be an emotionally rewarding experience, but it also requires a degree of commitment and stability that may not be achievable for a child who has never had such a caring experience themselves. Thus, expecting a child like this to look after an animal full time is not realistic. However, these children can still benefit from spending time with animals in a supervised way. For example, at a local dogs' home they can walk dogs, or at a cat sanctuary, groom cats. Taking part in an animal sponsorship scheme can also be therapeutic for a child in helping them to gain a sense of caring and responsibility, albeit at a distance.

But it is also important to recognise that for some children household animals often hold wholly different associations. While for many children pets can be sources of love and affection, for the children about whom we write there can be the association of abuse and cruelty. It is known that some people who abuse children have a history of hurting animals. Some abused children, neglected and uncared for, will have been hurt by a family pet or they will have witnessed an adult being cruel to an animal. Indirectly or directly, because animals may have been a part in a child's traumatic experiences, they can sometimes be associated with fear, pain and rage.

This does not mean that an abused child can have no connection with animals nor take pleasure in them. As well as what we say above about visits to a cat sanctuary or a dogs' home, staff members may occasionally bring in their own pets (though this should be ones, like dogs, and unlike, say, cats, that can be tethered or, like fish, can be contained).

In the course of their healing, traumatised children will become open to their own needs and progress from this to be able to empathise with and be concerned for the needs of others, including the needs of animals. There may well be a time in their own lives when they will choose to own a pet to which they will show consistent affection and which they will care for perfectly well.

The experience of a home as a home

A house is four walls, no matter how large or small it is, with however many rooms. The grandest of houses devoid of decoration and furniture look empty in the deepest sense. A home is a place where people live, where they enjoy one another's company, celebrate one another's triumphs and share one another's disappointments and help to make up for them.

What happens in the home (good and bad), in part, derives from how the house looks and the atmosphere it conveys. The experience of abused and often traumatised children who enter residential care means that those who create the home have to be all the more sensitive to the needs of those whose home it will be and mindful of those experiences it contains.

The physical circumstances and surroundings of where the child lives are in themselves a therapeutic opportunity. They are psychologically, as well as physically, significant. The home should be specifically designed to meet the needs of the children. There is a *total* effort concentrated on the child in the *total* environment in which the child now finds herself. This is because *every* part of a child's life is seen as having potential for therapy and, therefore, the home is structured in such a way that the everyday details reflect this.

Carole in the light: the sometimes extreme impact of environment

Until she was 11 years old, Carole had lived in a pub with her parents. She was sexually abused first by a paternal uncle, and later by her father also, while downstairs people were drinking, eating and talking. Her memories of the abuse were dominated by recollections of shouts and laughter from downstairs, and she would describe herself as having concentrated on these sounds whilst staring at the light coming from her bedroom windows.

Carole would sometimes think the noises from downstairs were people laughing and shouting at her, and she would say she felt safer when it was noisy downstairs, even when 'it' was happening. She had, however, little memory of the abuse itself which she could express verbally, perhaps because she had repressed much of it, or because her escape into the sounds from downstairs and the light from her bedroom window had effectively taken her outside any conscious experience of it happening.

Carole was removed from the care of her family and, after several short-term foster placements, she spent three years in a residential home, where she made considerable progress towards recovery.

She moved to a new foster placement when she was 14 and, almost immediately, became very low in mood, quiet and withdrawn, similar to how she had been three years previously.

Outside of Carole's bedroom in her new home was a bright, yellow street light, similar to the one close by the pub where she had once lived with her parents and where she had suffered abuse. She herself remarked on the similarity but dismissed a possible link between it and the rapid return of her feelings of being detached and depressed.

After a few weeks, Carole began to experience the type of violent rages which she had not had for over two years. She assaulted her foster mother, broke windows and destroyed her own belongings.

After careful discussion and persuasion, she agreed to change bedrooms, and the positive effect was almost as immediate and dramatic as the deterioration had been when she first arrived in the foster home. For Carole, the sensory association of the yellow light with her experience of abuse was much more powerful than she realised or was able to acknowledge.

Tommy, the boy with potatoes in his pockets: building recovery through simple, shared experience

Tommy, who was eight, lived with his parents and four half-brothers and sisters. When they sat and watched television, he was told that this or that programme was one he didn't like. At the home, he would spend most of the time in his sparsely furnished bedroom. When they sat down to eat, often sharing takeaways, he was told that the food would not be to his taste and he would be given different food, which was usually a piece of toast or a chocolate bar; sometimes it was nothing at all.

On the first day he arrived at the residential care home, Tommy refused to eat. He would not sit with the other children or even enter the dining room. He looked at the food that was taken to him but, even with encouragement, he would not be persuaded to taste it.

Later on that first evening, Tommy was seen going up the stairs with mashed potato in his pockets that he had taken from the leftovers in the kitchen. He was given a small plate of food in his bedroom, which he angrily threw out the door.

The only way in which Tommy would eat for the first time was if he was allowed to 'steal' food and take it to his room. In his room, he would sleep on the floor, not in the bed, and he would attempt to hide food items under the carpet.

Tommy was asked to join in at every meal time. He was fascinated by watching the children and adults sit and eat but would not sit down to participate. After almost a week, Tommy agreed to stand in the dining room and eat a sandwich. After another week, he ate at the table, but only if he was given smaller portions than the other children. Gradually, slowly, Tommy began to take his place and to join in with the routine of the meal time.

It took almost six months before Tommy was confident enough to choose his food and to stop attempting to hide food in his bedroom. By this time, he had also overcome his reluctance to sleeping in his bed. This acceptance of basic comfort and care was not an easy step for Tommy to take, but it was the beginning of building a sense of self-worth vital to his recovery.

CHAPTER 4

Another Kind of Parent

Therapeutic Parenting

To turn Philip Larkin's pessimistic words about parents on their head: when they mean to, your mum and dad, they help you to grow.[1] Love, warmth, security, nurture, consistency, protection and support – these are gifts that good parents give to their child and it is these which shape the healthy child who grows to become the well-adjusted and loving adult.

We call this nurturing, a word which resonates with the idea of time being committed to tending, with care and protectiveness, and enveloped by love and warmth, to create gradual, healthy growth. Aynsley-Green (2005) lists eight aspects of nurture as:

- love and care
- physical contact and comfort
- nutrition, warmth and protection from home
- security and stability
- play and exploration
- education
- friendships
- expectations and a purpose in life.

---

1   The first lines of Philip Larkin's poem, 'This be the Verse' are 'They fuck you up your mum and your dad./They may not mean to, but they do.'

Many children who enter a Restorative Parenting programme have suffered deprivations in some or all of these areas. In the most extreme cases, children who have been severely abused have been completely denied these things, which means their attachment is so disordered, their emotional development so disrupted and their trauma, such that trust of adults for them is impossible and they are unable to make relationships, as we have explained in Chapter 2. A child who has been damaged in this way requires a therapeutic parent. Put in the form of a simple equation, we can say that parenting + therapy = therapeutic parenting. We could call it parenting plus, and by that understand that it is good parenting informed by psychological knowledge and understanding of child development and the effects of trauma, theories of child development of how traumatised children act and react, and how the therapeutic parent deals with that.

Dockar-Drysdale (1990) also illustrates a practical distinction between good parenting and therapeutic parenting with the example of food, when she writes: '…therapeutic workers in residential work, while aiming to provide a balanced diet, are tuned to the emotional needs of the child where food is under consideration.'

So, while a good parent nurtures his child through growth and healthy development, a therapeutic parent is a staff member who has to repair the damage the child has sustained through neglect or abuse and lack of stability. However, repair such as this is not an event but a process which may begin immediately, but needs to continue over a long period of time.

Despite repeatedly experiencing a range of sometimes extreme emotions and behaviours, a child has to see that the relationship between her and the therapeutic parent remains positive and intact. There is no substitute for the child and the therapeutic parent sharing this lived experience of relationship building.

The relationship is about helping children to reach a level of stability that allows them to participate positively in everyday activities. This is a process of growth in which there are often many setbacks, each of which is an opportunity for the child to re-experience the return of positive acceptance, affection and trust. Gradually skills, that most children develop so naturally that they go almost unnoticed – such as conversational turn taking and the ability to enjoy positive interaction with others – begin to build. The child begins to be able consistently to do ordinary things like sleep well and eat easily with others. Through the process of restorative parenting, children are helped to lead lives close to those led by children who live at home with their families. They attend mainstream school, spend time with friends and take part in after-school clubs and a whole range of activities.

Therapeutic parenting is a means of compensating a child for what she lacked from her parents or early carers. Pughe and Philpot (2007) explain:

> Therapeutic parenting is a professional technique and, as such, is structured in the help that it offers, while giving as near as possible an approximation to the kind of positive parenting which a child should have received.

What is needed to be a therapeutic parent?

The work of a therapeutic parent is demanding, but can also be immensely satisfying. There can be few roles which carry such responsibility without being acknowledged as being truly professional in nature.

At a formal level, the employer should seek to establish a workforce with proven academic ability and a willingness to undertake further training and studies, potentially up to degree level and beyond. Informally, a certain amount of maturity and life experience can be enormously helpful. Good therapeutic parents can come from a wide range of backgrounds and bring varied skills and experience to the role. For example, Halliwell Homes employs someone who is a former hairdresser and someone else who was in the Royal Navy. This variation is important to meet the different expectations and interests of the children who enter the programme.

For those people in the role with a first degree, a home could also consider sponsoring further study right up to Ph.D. level, as Halliwell Homes does. Therapeutic child care is a valuable, vocational role, and therapeutic parents should be regarded as professional people in the same way that, for example, social workers and teachers are professionals.

People joining as therapeutic parents will work for a professional child care qualification – a Certificate in Restorative Parenting (CRP) – which can be completed up to degree level. This gives the therapeutic parent working knowledge of child development, attachment theory, childhood trauma, recovery processes and some relevant child psychiatry.

In addition to the CRP qualification, staff will also have applied training in matters like attention deficit hyperactivity disorder (ADHD), childhood epilepsy, bereavement, bullying, professionals working together, and safeguarding. Individual learning goals are also set, within a framework of personal and professional development, supported by regular supervision; participation in consultation; and the availability of counselling.

The acquisition of knowledge is about understanding children's needs in the context of child development; developmental possibilities; reflective experience; disrupted attachment; and trauma.

However, it is not enough to acquire knowledge. It is what restorative parenting calls 'the lived experience of the child'. The challenge is not arriving at a model or knowledge base but practising knowledge. The ability to do this will depend on how the agency is organised and operated, and how it is geared to a recovery model.

Taking the lessons of dynamic systems theory, the child and the process of recovery should never be seen in isolation. It should be remembered that staff, too, are important; they, too, need to be cared for, and they need also to care for themselves. They must allow time for themselves so that they can sleep easily and be prepared emotionally for the next day.

The greatest challenge that faces the therapeutic parent is to invest emotionally in, and be available to, the child; to engage the child so that, in turn, the child will not only learn to trust adults but also to realise why it is worth trusting in them. These are not just people doing a job or on shift or following a set of rules, but people working on a human level with a child. The adult, then, must be prepared to be there for the long term; a long-term commitment needs to be allied with emotional stability.

The ideal recruit will be someone who is resilient, empathetic, attentive, able, physically fit and willing to invest in the children, and have an ability to learn and develop a knowledge base about children. Enthusiasm, self-awareness and emotional literacy, as well as intellectual ability and good communication skills, are characteristics to be looked for in the therapeutic parent.

As referred to previously, there can sometimes be a tension between a system of governance based on rigorously applied procedures and the flexibility needed to therapeutically re-parent a child in a naturally responsive way.

Bethany: when a hug made school more difficult

Bethany, aged eight, was very excited about her first day at a new school. Planning meetings had ensured that the school was well aware of her needs and the fact of her being a looked-after child. On her first morning, one of her two key workers, James, took her to school and she threw her arms around him at the gate in a prolonged hug which James reciprocated. This was part of Bethany's usual behaviour, but had over the past year progressed from indiscriminate affection to being reserved only for those people she knew well.

A staff member at the school, knowing that James was not Bethany's parent, but a paid carer, expressed a safeguarding concern which was passed on to the local duty social worker. The direction from safeguarding was that James be suspended while the incident was investigated. This was done and, within a few days, with the formal processes complete, James returned to work without the need for any further action. However, James had not been available to greet Bethany after her first day at school as he had promised her. This damaged her trust in him and, because of her heightened vulnerability to such setbacks, her trust in other adults too. Bethany was helped to overcome this, but her transition to school was much more difficult than anticipated.

The demands of an overly risk-averse system should not limit what therapeutic parents can do and should not dictate a uniform practice. This needs to be guarded against, when child-centred practice demands spontaneity.

The therapeutic parent is someone who will celebrate a child's success and empathise with her disappointments and want to help to overcome those setbacks. In a literal sense this is someone who will give time and his emotional availability to stay with the child – this is not about overtime but the child's needs.

The therapeutic parent must always be a role model for a child, and that can be a way for her to learn that certain reactions are not necessarily negative. Take, for example, anger. Being angry with a child may not always be unprofessional – it may allow a child to see why anger can sometimes be permissible.

For example, a child of eight is out shopping with her therapeutic parent, and in the car park, as the shopping is being loaded into the car, like any parent, the therapeutic parent shouts 'Stop right there!' as the child walks away, distracted by something. The child, like any child, cries, and the parent says: 'You scared me – I thought you were going to wander off and there are cars around.' But, once they are in the car, the therapeutic parent gives the child a hug and the child realises that the therapeutic parent still loves her, but can also see why the therapeutic parent shouted – because he was worried about the child.

In this instance, too, the therapeutic parent was conscious of how his actions affected the child. The need is then to re-engage with the child as quickly as possible and be conscious of the child's level of arousal. It may be appropriate to apologise and to say something like 'That was not about you', or to make a gesture, like a cuddle, which is what happened. In certain circumstances, depending on the nature of the incident, the next steps may require clinical advice or supervision.

However, there should be no withdrawal of goodies as a punishment – like cancelling that trip to a match or the cinema. Going to the cinema or a match are positive, and should be maintained so long as the therapeutic parent, given the nature of the incident, with the support available, is able to deal with this emotionally.

What kind of person is a therapeutic parent?

We have discussed above some of the qualities needed to be a successful therapeutic parent. But choosing and, perhaps more importantly, retaining the right people can be a challenge.

For restorative parenting to be effective, the children need consistency, and this is partly dependent on the retention of staff, which is always a challenge (see below). Some graduates, for example, want to travel or may be looking to broaden their experience without having decided upon any particular career path. A better candidate will be someone who has already done this. Retention is inextricably linked to selection, but thought must be given not only to who is to be recruited, but how they are paid and rewarded; what educational opportunities will be made available to them; and what are the appropriate levels of support to be offered for the role the new recruit is to undertake.

There is a detailed application form and then an intensive first interview with the lead therapeutic parent, which will involve the presentation of likely practice scenarios. There will also be shadowing or working alongside experienced therapeutic parents for a day or two. Then second interviews attempt to gain applicants' impressions, which can lead to an appointment as a trainee therapeutic parent (as well, of course, as weeding out those who realise that this is not a job for them).

Retaining staff

The problem of the retention of staff besets most care providers, but is particularly significant with regard to therapeutic parenting, because without the consistent support to build lasting relationships the therapeutic programme cannot be effective. Relationships between the therapeutic parent and the child are an essential element in the programme. Thus, the retention of a stable staff group is of the utmost – indeed, critical – importance.

A sense of ownership of the programme by the therapeutic parenting team, fostering a vocational commitment and a sense of values, helps to ensure that staff see their work as more than a matter of pay and conditions. This is not to say that tangible rewards are not important in retaining staff. To these must be added other important policies that can help retain staff: increasing their satisfaction and furthering their professional development. These would, as mentioned previously, include opportunities for further training and qualifications (through to higher education), but also travel, whether attending conferences at home and abroad or allowing time and expenses for study or related work elsewhere. It is important, too, that therapeutic parents who work in the home develop an expertise sufficient that they are able to work alongside the education and clinical teams, as well as feel part of the whole programme, with an ability and interest to contribute to its quality.

The essence of therapeutic parenting

As we noted in Chapter 2, restorative parenting is an approach that has adapted, developed and combined a number of elements to create its overall model. Maginn (2006) makes an important distinction which goes to the heart of therapeutic parenting when he distinguishes between 'caring for a child' and 'caring about a child'.

The therapeutic parent is a substitute parent for the child and must care about her with a similar depth of genuine care and affection. The care provided must be informed by additional knowledge and understanding, reflecting the needs of children who have suffered trauma, but, without the fundamental emotional warmth of genuine caring, no amount of clinically informed practice will successfully help a child regain the capacity to trust which their experience has taken away.

We have referred previously to the role of individual therapy in the Restorative Parenting programme. It is surprising to us that while a child is traumatised experientially, there is such a widely held assumption that recovery can occur discretely through the mechanism of individual therapy. Restorative parenting works at the level of the child's lived experience, as it is only in the wholeness of experience that recovery is to be found.

The traumatised abused child may communicate through her behaviour what she cannot put into words, and the therapeutic parent must be constantly watchful to understand what is being 'said'. In response, the adult's actions 'tell' the child that adults can be people who care and protect and that relationships need not necessarily be abusive ones – that it is safe for the child to trust again.

Good parents tend often to act spontaneously in caring for their children. That is a natural way of acting as a parent, and therapeutic parents will also act spontaneously at times. However, therapeutic parenting is a professional role and, as such, is necessarily somewhat structured in the help that it offers, while giving as near as possible an approximation to the kind of positive parenting which a child should have received.

Therapeutic parenting is not a passive activity, any more than the child is a passive receiver: it is about actively building and maintaining relationships, between individuals and those to be experienced in groups, when people live together. It is about giving and receiving and what that may positively lead to.

Restorative parenting actively creates a consistent, responsive, nurturing context, on an interpersonal and environmental level, that allows the child to regain a sense of security. Through this process the child builds corrective attachments which to a degree compensate for what she has previously been denied. This will allow her to trust, to form relationships with others, and to develop her own sense of self, as well as a growing understanding of the needs of others and her part in that, both by the impact she has on others, and how with healthy maturity she will come to help meet those needs of others.

This latter aspect is attached to the child's emerging understanding of what it is to live in a community, that others have needs, too, that there is give and take and compromise. This will parallel the growth of empathy on the child's part. Ultimately, assisted by the therapeutic parent in a therapeutic environment, the child will be able to move successfully to family placement and, eventually, to the realisation of herself as a loving and responsible person.

Jackie's fond farewell

There were three trainee therapeutic parents in the home from which Jackie was to move. It was her last day before moving to a foster home, and, at that time, she was at school. The trainees objected to clearing up Jackie's room, which was in a bit of a mess and all her belongings were stacked in black bin bags. It was not their job, they said; they were not cleaners. But leaving somewhere, for a child like Jackie, had memories of being taken into care and associations of loss, unhappiness and uncertainty about the future.

The lead therapeutic parent spoke to the trainees, explaining how she would perceive her room on her last day when she returned from school – how different, it was suggested, it would be if Jackie's room could be tidied and her belongings properly and neatly packed. It would give Jackie a sense of being valued, of people caring about her departure. The trainees saw the point and set to work. They also had her favourite tea ready for her and bought a card, which they all signed, wishing her the best for her future. In this way, cleaning and tidying up had been a way to help Jackie make her move more confidently and happily, while turning a standard job into a therapeutic task for the trainees.

This reflects an important element of the programme – that what might appear mundane and routine can be mindfully therapeutic if considered part of the child's lived experience.

CHAPTER 5

It's the Relationship that Counts

When we say that a child needs therapy we do so on the assumption that contact with the therapist will allow the child to gain insight into her condition and change. Such an assumption is, however, flawed. First, because it assumes that the child has no other influences upon her behaviour, whereas, in fact, she is subject to a host of divergent and differing influences. But, second, it unfairly places responsibility for change on the child.

Of course, there is sometimes value in working individually with a child to help them to process thoughts and feelings which they might otherwise find it difficult or impossible to do. But, too often, the assumption is that such individual 'therapy' is a means by which the child can be helpfully changed so as to be able to cope with traumatic life experiences, stressful relationships and toxic environments. However, a child should not be expected to adjust their thoughts and feelings as an individual as a means of recovery. To develop and grow through the actual experience of positive relationships, participation, involvement and engagement within a safe and fully nurturing environment is the means by which lasting recovery can be achieved. It is the responsibility of adults entrusted with the care of the child to provide and maintain this context, and we should not expect any form of structured therapy to mitigate for the lack of it.

Thus, the recovery programme is one which surrounds the children with therapy by creating the therapeutic environment which we described in Chapter 3. It is important, however, that if children are to benefit fully from the programme and it is to be effective, then staff (that is, the therapeutic practice team) should have ownership of the programme. If not, they are not only hampered in their ability to help the child, but also their dissatisfaction can influence the whole environment, which itself will, apart from other effects, have an impact upon the child.

Therapeutic parents need to know what the programme aspires to do and why and how, and why it is better than other programmes in achieving its aims. One therapeutic parent, Diana Jepson, explained to us:

> Working with the model is important – it's very different from how it was. Without the model it was more about child minding, now it's doing something to make a difference for a child. It used to be almost natural for children to get a criminal record – expectations of 'care kids' were low, whereas as now it's about getting a good education, going into foster care; good outcomes are the way now. It's almost like we look after our children now as though they were our own. It's a home, not just a house. We work hard with our children, want the best for them.

The therapeutic practice team are the ones who interact with the child. It is they who provide the home, the support and the feeling of being loved and cared for that each child needs and that is fundamental to their recovery. The commitment and understanding needed is amply demonstrated in Diana Jepson's description, and such ownership of the process is actively supported clinically, managerially and, indeed, through the whole structure of the organisation.

The lack of ownership which therapeutic parents can sometimes feel can arise for many reasons. One, for example, is a problem – say, divorce, the breakdown of a relationship, or bereavement – arising in the personal life of a staff member. The therapeutic parent can sometimes unavoidably bring what he is feeling in such situations – say, the sadness and resentment – into the home. This can impact directly on that person's ability to work therapeutically in the way required of the programme. His emotional stability may be temporarily impaired in a way which may not be obvious but can still have an adverse impact on sensitive and vulnerable children.

There is a responsibility on all members of the team to actively support and, to a degree, monitor their colleagues to ensure they remain focussed and emotionally aware in carrying out the role of therapeutic parenting.

During everyday interactions, the challenge for the practice team, the supervisory process and, if necessary, the additional support of counselling services is to help a colleague experiencing personal life stresses to continue to function well in the therapeutic parenting role. Sometimes a break away from the home can be helpful, but this needs to be managed carefully, bearing in mind the vulnerability of the children to perceived as well as actual rejection.

Sometimes a glitch in the way the programme is working or some perceived shortcoming in the programme can seem to some individuals to be a major problem, which can then have wider repercussions. But the ripples of these repercussions can spread further – a complaint to Ofsted or a negative remark to an inspector, for example, may have little basis in fact, but nevertheless raises questions and sometimes concerns. This can set in motion processes of enquiry and investigation – such as additional visits by Ofsted and so on – which, while often not a major problem in themselves, do disrupt the routine of the home to a degree and can impact on the lived experience of the child.

For this to happen, the therapeutic parent may not have been adequately supported. This is likely to further disrupt the child's lived experience.

Another way in which ownership is not taken is when someone joins the team from another agency, with his own view of how things should be done. He believes that his method of working is superior to that of the programme and, in some cases, attempts to adapt the programme to his ideas or, in some cases, to impose his ideas and way of working on others. (This is not to say, of course, that a restorative parenting programme is static: it must always be open and responsive to other ideas and to evolve, but the decisive criterion must always be – how does any change or adaptation affect the welfare of the child? Does it contribute or detract from the therapeutic nature of the lived experience?)

Therapeutic parents taking ownership of the programme is not an episode or an event but a process, which is absorbed by them into an understanding about how they perceive the children and work with them. This taking ownership means that the therapeutic model is adhered to by everyone, and such consistency is essential for working with a child like Jane.

Jane: when school's out

Jane was 11 and the only child of her parents, both of whom are alcoholics. The degree of their inebriation tended to influence their reactions to their daughter, either on the part of one of them or, sometimes, both of them. Thus, when Jane came home from school, sometimes her parents – who drank all day and every day – would greet her affectionately, have her sit with them on the sofa, cuddle her, and ask her about her day. Sometimes their affection, induced by their inebriated state, became overly emotional and all three would sit crying together. But at other times, they could ignore her. And at yet other times, they could act with random violence toward her, or verbally abuse her. Jane never knew what to expect when she came through the door. While they'd always been drunk, their behaviour toward her became chronically neglectful when she was about six or seven and she took on the responsibility of getting herself ready for school each morning. She would also try to look after her parents by doing housework and by supporting an image of them as capable and caring. Despite the lack of nurture, even basic care, she was given, Jane remained intensely loyal to her parents.

Consistency and inconsistency and the consequences

The Russian Ivan Pavlov and the American B. S. Skinner (Bjork, 1997) both demonstrated ideas about consistency and reaction to rewards, with their experiments in conditioning with, respectively, dogs and rats. How animals react to being offered food in different ways – consistently and inconsistently, regularly and irregularly –

and to the amounts offered (including none at all) – and what they will do to obtain food are well documented and familiar to students of psychology.

Many behavioural psychology studies explain the basics of stimulus–reinforcement and reward schedules. For our purposes it is enough to recall that if a subject doesn't know how much, if any, reward a particular behaviour may produce, or when that reward might come, the behaviour is powerfully conditioned and difficult to remove. This is the same dynamic which conditions problem gambling – the reward is uncertain, both in terms of the amount there will be and when or if it will be achieved. Every bet comes with hope attached, and many, many disappointments do not detract from the belief that a big reward may be just one more bet away.

Behavioural psychology offers an insight into the reaction of human beings to (in)consistency. Consistency for all children is paramount – it allows them to know how to react and in what way and to whom, and, thus, importantly, whom they can trust. Traumatised children, by the nature of what has happened to them, have not known consistency. If we accept that children are goal-orientated (even if, sometimes, the goals are negative – for example, the intention is to run away), then they meet problems when they find inconsistency in reaction to achieving those goals.

But when we talk about consistency, we mean that it needs to meet matters large and small, and that to be experienced as reliable, and as trustworthy, therapeutic parents should have similar, if not always the same, reactions. It is natural that one therapeutic parent will have a better relationship with a certain child than a colleague, but that does not mean that the actions and reactions of the two therapeutic parents should be inconsistent when it comes to the child. If a child swears, there will be therapeutic parents who do not accept that, but there will be others who find it acceptable. The consistency here, as elsewhere, comes both through ownership of the programme by all members of the team, but also the quality of the relationships within the team.

It is natural that we should seek the best possible reaction on the part of staff, but it is better to have two less than optimal but consistent approaches, than one which is the best possible and an entirely different one which is also potentially ideal, because the two in combination make for inconsistency. Take, for example, a child who screams loudly demanding an adult's attention. It may be an effective response partly to engage with the child and request that she doesn't shout so loudly. It may also be effective to ignore the screaming and wait for a less challenging approach. It could be that providing the child with lots of reassurance and close, calming support would also work well. Which is the best response will depend upon the needs of the particular child, but what is clear from learning theory is that the inconsistency of all three responses – used at different times – will not be helpful at all. If a child does not know what response her behaviour will receive – whether the result will be success (attention in our example) or failure, to what degree, and for how long – then the behaviour will continue.

In a home where a child has suffered abuse, inconsistency can occur when those who have mistreated children have not been wholly negative in their attitudes toward them – that, at least, would have been consistent – but they have, at times, been positive toward them and, at other times, indifferent. The adults have treated the child sometimes abusively and sometimes affectionately, and so the child does not know what to expect and therefore how to react.

Few parents are completely negative toward their children; when they are, the children are often abandoned. But abusive parents can also show love to their child. However, while negative experiences overshadow the positive ones, these different parental reactions are why, very often, an abused child retains a loyalty to the parent. She does not want to lose the parent; what she wants is for the abuse to stop. But one result of inconsistency is that a child's behaviour will not change, and neither can it be expected to, even with therapy, nor can she be expected to take responsibility for that change.

Therapy is not enough to re-build the capacity for trust, because the child must experience consistency in the environment in which she lives, offered by those who work with her. The child who has experienced adult responses as inconsistent and unreliable, and therefore untrustworthy, must have a different, corrective, experience in order to overcome behaviour patterns which are self-defeating, but fixed and difficult to change. This is the total environment, the 24-hour lived experience of the child; therapy is something which must surround her, as we said above and have explained in detail in Chapter 3.

Carrie: lessons about consistency

When Carrie was in residential care, she behaved in a very challenging way at times, whereas at other times she could be very kind and caring. After school, she would create problems – sometimes she would be physically violent to other children or the team, and sometimes she would abuse them verbally. This expressed her anxiety and lack of trust in others. Carrie had come from a home in which both her parents were alcoholics and drug users. She had feared coming home from school, never knowing what she was going to encounter. Her challenging behaviour did not show itself at school because school for her had always been a place of safety, where she met consistent reactions. Thus, she needed to experience consistency in the home that was positive and explicit. Through this she came to see that people could be consistent, were there for her and, therefore, could be trusted.

First impressions

We all find change stressful. A change from the familiar to the unknown is inherently difficult. For adults, a change in a relationship or a house move (not that either of these do not, of course, also affect children) can be highly stressful, not least because inconsistency is inherent in both experiences: what we think is intended to happen – say, the signing of the contract for the house move on a certain day – doesn't happen or is delayed. For children, the first day at school or, later, the transition from primary to secondary school are well known for being stressful.

The traumatised child has, through her treatment at the hands of adults, suffered high levels of stress and, at a time of transition (for example, the move to residential care), she has a heightened stress response, geared to react if something, almost anything, is out of place or happens in a way that is unexpected. The transition is stressful in itself, but the child can easily suffer re-traumatisation if the process happens without adequate preparation or does not proceed as planned. For example, she is told that on a certain day, at a certain time, she will meet someone from the home to which she is going to move. She is told who she will meet, where she will meet them and where the home is, and may have been given a photograph of the home. She is told that she can ask questions and also what kind of information will be given to her. In this situation, with everything planned and much expected, the potential of that heightened stress response if something goes wrong is magnified. This can so easily happen even with something as (unfortunately) routine as a change in the staff member who is to meet the child. 'Hello, Susie, I'm Liz – I'm afraid that Kaye couldn't be here today, so I've come' is not for the child the friendly and welcoming greeting that Liz intends it to be, and Susie will react accordingly. Part of the ownership of the programme, which we have discussed above, is the team being aware of just how significant to a traumatised child such seemingly small things can be.

Long-term relationships

There needs to be explicit acknowledgement among the therapeutic practice team that not all negative experiences can be avoided (for example, Kaye, in that last example, may not be able to make the meeting because her son has had to be absent from school due to sickness). But it is equally important that all staff strive to see that such experiences are minimised.

One of the most common negative experiences impacting upon a child is if a member of the therapeutic parenting team leaves. Few people stay in one place all their working life (and, in most cases, nor should they). People leave to further their careers, to give more time to their own children, or because a partner's job takes them to live elsewhere.

Thus, if someone leaves the team, the team must realise and accept the responsibility for the fact that the child will be set back by this and that the distress caused can be significant. This often means understanding that the child can regress back to an earlier stage of recovery. Routines that had been established can break down, and challenging behaviours that had been eliminated can reoccur. It is important that the practice team understand and appreciate that these reactions are not indications of recovery having gone irretrievably backwards or failed in some way. The emotional response of a child to the loss of a significant relationship with a trusted adult can often be more pronounced in those children who have made the greatest progress. The expression of upset, anger and sadness shows not only the level of distress a child is experiencing at the time, but also a certain trust in the context of care in which she lives.

The role of biological parents

Very often there are two lots of biological parents – those who actually exist and those who reside in the child's mind, that is, whom the child remembers or wishes them to be. Here there exists a tension which many professionals seek to reconcile to the disadvantage of the child. This is because they seek to deny what the child remembers positively about her parents – they are, after all, the authors of her problems. For example, Jane (see her case study on page 73) would send elaborate birthday cards to her parents. 'She shouldn't do that', staff would say. For them, the parents had abused her and landed her where she was. This was true, but Jane also remembered the affection her parents showed her and their interest in what she'd done in school some days.

Let us take another situation, which concerned ten-year-old Jamie and his mother. She had suffered severe depression and, on contact days, Jamie would be the one taking the lead in the conversation, thinking about what they would talk about, and sometimes the response was only a blank stare. The staff believed that this was a burden for Jamie and so contact should be stopped. It *was* a burden for him, but it had to be set against his wish to see his mother because he had a positive view of her, which staff could not see.

Sometimes a child's positive concept of their parents can seem to be completely immune to the negative experiences and disappointments that they inflict upon them. Multiple failures to live up to contact agreements, broken promises and even callous rejections can somehow be overlooked in favour of the 'ideal parent' which dwells in the child's mind.

Take, for example, Zac's mother. She was supposed to attend supervised contact with him once a month. She would often write short letters to him saying how much she was looking forward to seeing him and would confirm her attendance with his social worker the day before Zac got himself ready and travelled the 100 miles to meet her at the appointed time. Almost always, she would be late, and half the time she wouldn't show up at all. Sometimes Zac's mother would apologise for not being there – more often she would make up some excuse that blamed miscommunication from the local authority. On three occasions in the space of a few months, Zac's mother blamed him for her predicaments of housing and relationship problems and said that she would never see him again. Zac would be upset every time such things happened, but he would quickly return to the positive view of his mother as a loving and capable parent who was prevented from looking after him by faceless and uncaring officials.

Reconciling the reality of parental rejection and failure with the positive recollections or fantasy of the ideal parent figure the child wishes to have is a difficult and lengthy process which may never be fully achieved. Even in adulthood, the person who has grown up in care may still hope the rejecting parent will become the supportive and reliable figure they had always wanted.

It is common for adults who look after children in care to feel antipathy towards the parents who they observe to be rejecting and uncaring towards their children. Often there will be calls for contact to be restricted or stopped because of it, particularly when the child is obviously disturbed by the experience. However, a cessation of contact is rarely helpful, and a great deal of effort needs to be made to agree and support a contact arrangement which is as reliable as possible. This may mean the contact being less frequent and shorter. There may need to be strict timings and supervision arrangements, but keeping some contact with a parent is often invaluable to a child's eventual recovery – even if only because it helps with the process of reconciling, to whatever degree is possible, the fantasy parent figure with the reality of experience and expectation.

Other people in a child's life

There are other adults outside the home who impinge on children's lives and their lived experience and where care has to be taken that that experience is not disrupted. In Chapter 8 we discuss how police, Ofsted inspectors, social workers, GPs and health staff can have an impact on the children and the home's regime.

Relationships within residential care are critical; they are a key therapeutic element in the programme. Dysfunctional and abusive relationships are why the child is where she is and have created the need for the treatment she is receiving. Restorative parenting is a re-parenting process, but fundamentally it is a means of remaking a healthy relationship with children which they can experience as reliable and trustworthy.

Joy: the little girl who became a little adult

Before Joy came to the home, when she was ten, she'd not merely adopted the persona of an adult, she acted like one and tried to pass herself off as one. She smoked, wore makeup and dressed in high heels and short skirts; she even put socks down the front of her tops to give the impression of having a bust. When she came to the home she expressed her 'adulthood' by trying to 'parent' other children.

In the two years that Joy had been at the home, she'd been helped to become the child she really was and, importantly, to accept that that was what she was: she gave up smoking, makeup, high heels and short skirts. In the course of this change, she had established good relationships with three adults who worked with her. Kay was one adult in particular with whom she got on exceptionally well, but Kay left the home when she found a team manager's job elsewhere. This was a trigger for Joy to revert to some of her past behaviour – importantly, her 'parenting' of other children. She would also destroy treats for children and then attempt to rectify what had happened by trying to make up to them, to comfort them for what had gone wrong, as a parent would. So, for example, at one child's birthday party, Joy destroyed the cake and the goodies and threw over the chairs set at the table. Then she attempted to send the other children to bed and tried to comfort the child whose birthday party it was.

Joy's reversion was caused by the loss she experienced at Kay's leaving. She required one-to-one help, the chance to engage in activities which she enjoyed, and intensive reassurance and support – all within the totality of the therapeutic environment in which she lived. This enabled staff to make positive attributions (see Chapter 2) so that Joy's behaviour was not seen as pathological.

Thus, staff took responsibility for effecting change in Joy – they did not expect that to be something for which she was responsible. As we have said above, the other response to her behaviour would be to say that she required therapy to express her feelings and gain insight into why she acted as she did, and so would have placed that responsibility for change on her.

CHAPTER 6

A Matter of Choices

Clinical Insight for the Long Term

By the time a child enters foster care, she will have made significant progress through restorative parenting and the programme that we have described in earlier chapters. Fostering is a new stage in her life, but it is not, in some ways, a different stage. This is because it is a continuation and reinforcement of what has gone before, and foster carers will be helped to practise the values and concepts of the programme. Thus, this chapter applies to those working with traumatised children in whatever context and at whatever stage the child has reached.

While promoting clinically informed long-term lifestyle choices is not peculiar to foster care because within the programme therapeutic parents, teachers and others will already have undertaken this, the focus in a foster family will be necessarily somewhat different. By the time a child enters foster care, she will have greater self-awareness, have developed self-management skills and substantially increased emotional resilience. The focus in foster care moves increasingly towards facilitation and guidance, and the approach is more flexible in its application. By the time she enters foster care, the child will also be able to make her own choices with the help and support of her foster parents. She will be able to hold a longer-term perspective, having overcome the reactive, short-term decision-making that tends to characterise children in the early stages of recovery. This is not to say that she does not retain vulnerability, as we shall explain.

Prompting clinically informed long-term lifestyle choices is an approach to behaviour management in which expected stresses are dealt with by bringing to them a clinical understanding. Let us take, as an example, the case where a child falls out with a group of other children at school. In ordinary circumstances a parent might talk about this with the child and, where he felt that bullying might be involved, then might speak to the class teacher. While bullying (if, indeed, that was happening) can have serious consequences, most childish falling out has no long-term effect. The child gets through it, friendships form and re-form, and this will most likely be no more than a blip on a child's progress through school.

But with a child who has suffered trauma, talking about what has happened is not likely to be enough of a solution, because rejection by other children (as with rejection by adults) has the potential to reawaken previous vulnerabilities. What might be a mild setback for another child has the potential to be very serious for the kind of children that we are writing about. Restorative parenting builds resilience in these children, but they remain more than averagely sensitive to experiencing further feelings of rejection and, for a time at least, they are at increased risk of becoming re-traumatised.

The still vulnerable child

The way a once-traumatised child responds to an issue like that described above happens more quickly, can be greater in effect, and that effect can continue for longer than would be the case with another child. Thus, the need is for adults to intervene quickly to offer more support, and to recognise that the support may have to continue for longer than might otherwise be the case.

The child who has suffered trauma will have a greater than average need for consistency and she will be more than usually vigilant in detecting any perceived inconsistency. However, that said, there is nothing static about a child's condition. Her ability to deal with inconsistency, as with other problems she meets, will improve over time.

The ability to cope with stress is, in part, for all of us, the ability to cope with ambiguity, but for the traumatised child her tolerance of ambiguity will be that much lower. Her sensitivity to actual or perceived ambiguity will often centre on relationships. Does her foster parent really care for her? Does he really love her? Other children may see indications towards a negative answer to those questions (or musings, we might say, for children may not ask questions explicitly but keep them inside themselves) as transitory, but resting upon a fundamental assurance that the carer does care for her and does love her. But for the traumatised child what is transitory for others may take on the appearance of being permanent if the perception is not dealt with and the child reassured.

Children who come into care will often have been disengaged from education, and some will have been involved with the criminal justice system. These factors are well recognised as a continued risk for children who pass through the care system. The danger, then, is that a setback in the recovery programme can cause the child to become disengaged from education again and to fall in with others similarly disengaged who may also be involved with the police or likely to become so. Restorative parenting offers nurturing and a sense of belonging, but a child who becomes detached can be led to old situations of, for example, chronically refusing school or being exploited by gangs.

When a child is not doing well at school or is finding problems in making relationships with other children and adults that are based on trust (the two will often be linked), then these alternatives may seem attractive. What the child has to be helped to see is that the right choice is one where short-term gains are not purchased at the cost of the prospects for a long-term, positive lifestyle.

Restorative parenting is a means to help a child open up her choices. The most obvious (to the child) means of self-protection is not to trust adults or engage with them, not to dress appropriately, not to eat well and healthily, not to work, and to seek the company of others who do the same and to stay away from other children who do not. But what are the positive alternatives, the positive choices that the child can make? They obviously exist, but restorative parenting is not about telling or even gently encouraging a child not to act in these negative ways, but rather it is to help to build her self-esteem and a sense of self-worth so that she can see that the choices she makes today have their effect on her future. The child cannot acquire a long-term perspective or a balanced view by being directed to do so. Such an approach would be self-defeating, as it would simply feed into the reactive, negative and defensive state which prevents real recovery. The Restorative Parenting programme is not concerned with directing children on how to behave through the imposition of strict rules and sanctions. That would be in many ways a much easier task, but it would not equip the child with the skills she needs to make positive lifestyle choices for herself. It would not help her to develop emotionally, to recover.

It is no good saying to a child, 'Do you not know what will happen in the long term if you go on like this?', because no child, traumatised or otherwise, can see very far ahead, often no more than a few days, and a week may seem an unattainable prospect. Children live in the moment; they do not plan or envisage their long-term future in any detail.

Traumatised children retain some of their vulnerability, even though by now they have gone through residential care and restorative education and are in a mainstream school and settled in a foster home. Here the temptation, when problems arise, can be to go back to the short-term, reactive way of living, especially when a negative peer group exerts its pull on that child.

Trauma destroys a child's sense of self-worth, leaving her with a sense that she does not matter and thus that her future has no value. But when a child re-develops self-worth, she can see that the future matters because she matters, as does her place within the world.

For many children who have suffered trauma, the vulnerability and sense of rejection which they feel can be lifelong, although they learn to cope and live with it. However, life is about learning, and no less so for a child who has been through the care system. She, too, can learn from her experiences and can grow because of that. This learning does not cease when the child leaves the residential phase of the Restorative Parenting programme. By that time, she will have skills to cope – a sense of self-worth and greater emotional stability and resilience, but, as we have seen, she will still be in need of the right kind of help and guidance.

Working with foster carers

If an agency has its own fostering service, then the training of its own fostering carers, in terms of concepts and values, ought to be as one with the training given to those in other parts of the agency

– those who work in residential care and therapy. But even where the agency does not have this fostering arm, it is still possible to help foster carers, who will be contracted from local authorities or independent fostering agencies, to absorb the values and concepts of restorative parenting. This is most often achieved by a package of training, consultation and support agreed around the needs of the child. In some instances, this will mean continuing communication and support between the programme and foster parents for some considerable time.

Communication and provision of support can mean a range of things. For example, the Restorative Parenting programme can offer transitional support packages involving a tutorial-type education element for foster carers and support workers, behaviour management training, consultation, outreach support and even respite care. In some situations, while the child obviously lives in the foster home, the restorative parent can offer support by, say, taking the child to school or collecting her.

Such working together means that restorative parenting has to be adaptable; it is not about colonising another agency's concepts and values but being complementary to them, avoiding inconsistencies and teaching foster carers skills that do not contradict existing practices. It is often possible to recognise similar concepts in different programmes, though they may be hidden by different labels.

Cliché though it may be, we do all learn by our mistakes. It is a sign of increasing maturity that doing something wrong makes us reflect on how to avoid that situation in future and get it right next time. This is a never-ending process into old age because new situations, large and small, confront us all the time, but some are specific to the age we are.

It is in learning from our mistakes, in part, that our personality is shaped, and our identity established. If we do not learn in this way, then progress unravels, and no more so than for a child who has suffered trauma. However, it is important that while she must be helped to make informed and positive long-term choices, her negative behaviour must be seen to be symptomatic of trauma and not treated as a pernicious choice that she has made.

Natalie: a choice to smoke had positive results

Natalie was 14 when she moved into a foster home after spending 26 months in a residential home. She was in mainstream schooling and had aspirations to work with animals as a veterinary nurse. Her foster parents were a nurse and a health promotions worker. After four weeks of being in the foster home, Natalie began smoking, surreptitiously at first, but gradually more defiantly. She was excluded from school for three days along with two other girls for smoking in the building, and she also began smoking in her bedroom at home. Natalie argued with her foster parents about it to the point where she began to ask to leave.

Through the process of joint consultation it was agreed that it was Natalie's choice to smoke, but if she wanted help to stop she only had to ask. There were, of course, rules and choices attached to smoking that applied to everyone. School had to follow the law, so smoking in the building was not allowed, and, if Natalie chose to do so, she was, in effect, choosing not to be in school. Smoking was also expensive, and Natalie could be helped to decide what she wouldn't buy in order to be able to afford cigarettes. Because, as Natalie agreed, smoking was bad for one's health, people who cared about her wouldn't pay her extra money to do it. Using the principles of restorative parenting, Natalie was given the choice and reassured that, whatever her decision, her foster parents had made a commitment to her and that she was wanted and cared for. Her decision to smoke and responsibility for the choices around it were her own. The focus then shifted back to promoting the things that Natalie enjoyed doing and was successful and/or ambitious about – her education, her swimming club and her voluntary work at the local dogs' home. The smoking was hardly talked about and, after a while, Natalie quietly gave it up. A confrontation, with all the potential connotations of rejection playing into Natalie's vulnerabilities, had been avoided.

In the example of Natalie, it would have been all too easy to see her decision to start smoking as a direct challenge to her foster parents who were both health care professionals. In some ways it probably was, but as a test of their commitment to her, reflecting her need to be reassured. What could have been construed as a problem became a choice, leading to reassurance and a learning opportunity.

It is important too that, when the child is attending mainstream school, communication between the programme and the school is open and continuing, and not simply reactive to when something goes wrong (see Chapter 7).

Restorative parenting seeks to meet the whole child, at different stages of her development, not least when she regresses. Her progress, like life itself, will not be a smooth and unhindered path. But she will achieve maturity and make her own choices eventually, not through admonition or exhortation, but through the growth of her sense of self. She will come to see that there is a future for her and that she is worthy of it. She will come to this realisation more easily, helped by a foster parent with an informed understanding and perspective, not just by knowledge of the child herself, but also the way in which she has been and continues to be, affected by her experience. Such clinically informed insights in practice can help support the child to make the right choices and develop her potential.

CHAPTER 7

Education, Education, Education

A loving home creates healthy and well-adjusted human beings, who have the potential to make satisfactory, healthy relationships with others, both as children and adults. And the other necessary gift that we receive as children is a good, wide-ranging education. This prepares us for the world, but it also draws out our potential and opens us up to learning, discovering, understanding and enjoying the world.

Restorative parenting, as we have shown, is about re-parenting children who have been denied a consistent healthy and loving upbringing. Some have suffered the additional trauma of abuse, but all have experienced failures of parenting, which causes profound damage. Repairing that damage and healing the wounds are the essence of the recovery programme.

But this is not to neglect their education, which must be part of the programme if we are to reach the whole child. Children also learn from the moment they enter the world – the colours on the walls of the nursery, their parents' first words to them, which encourage their own first sounds, or their examination of shape and substance as they grip a parent's finger or try to hold a rattle. And, while we never cease to learn in an informal way, later, through nursery school and the education system and, for some, into higher education, our learning is also formal and, in its later stages, what we choose to learn about is partly stimulated by interest and partly to help us achieve ambitions.

A child who enters the Restorative Parenting programme may well have had a very patchy education – at school some days, on others, not, with frequent absence, sometimes through her own doing by absconding from school. Without consistent support and guidance from emotionally engaged parents, the educational engagement of the child is often limited even when they are present in school. Concerns and anxieties about home life, poor sleep, poor nutrition, a lack of confidence and difficulties in managing routines and coping with demands can limit, even prevent, a child's ability to engage with the curriculum. For some children, school itself can seem to be an irrelevance.

There are other children for whom school can be a sanctuary – a place of safety away from the threat and unpredictability of an abusive family situation. Sometimes a child can find a sense of nurture and support in school which may be entirely lacking at home, as the case of Paul shows.

Paul: when school is the carer

Paul was eight years old and lived with his mother and stepfather, both of whom were chronic problem drinkers. He attended the local primary school, and many concerns were raised by the staff about the standard of care he was receiving at home. His hygiene was poor and his clothes were dirty and often unsuitable for the weather. Social workers were closely involved with the family, and at times Paul's care did improve, but his parents, compromised as they were by their drinking, had great difficulty in consistently placing Paul's needs above their own. His class teacher would sometimes buy clothes for Paul, but his parents would sometimes become angry if they thought people were treating them 'like a charity'. Paul had a coat, PE kit, a towel and some basic toiletries that he kept at school. For his birthday, his teacher bought him a book with lots of pictures about elephants – his favourite animal. Paul's mother was disparaging, saying there was no need to buy him a book at all as he already had one.

Paul moved for a time to live with his maternal grandmother, but she was unable to continue to care for him and he returned home briefly, before going first to a short-term foster placement and then to another placement which was too far away from his school for him to carry on attending. Paul absconded on two occasions, the second time in an attempt to get to school. Three months later, after another foster placement breakdown, Paul came into residential care. For him, school had been his safety net, and without it, and having left home, his fragile sense of security had collapsed. However, the sense of being cared at school was a protective experience, the benefits of which remained to help speed his recovery.

And so, either as an essential remedial step or as a continuation of a reassuring experience, restorative parenting necessarily contains restorative education. This is not only about the provision of a good quality education for children, but it is also about helping children to trust and, in the immediate term, this is learning to trust teachers and other staff. Teachers are, then, very obviously providing education, but there is no division between what they do and what home staff do, in that both are, in their own ways, contributing to the therapeutic lived experience and are integral to the child's recovery.

Restorative education is about ensuring that whatever children have lost by the time they get to the home is recovered or, for many, learned for the first time. Thus, education plays an indispensable part in the work. But, of course, how traumatised children are taught and by whom, and the environment in which their teaching takes place, does not, at least in the first instance before entering mainstream education, accord exactly with the ordinary school. But because the transition to mainstream school will be made, it remains important that the programme's educational regime is tailored to help the child accommodate and adapt progressively to the environment she will find later, so that her transition can be as smooth as possible, with the fewest possible surprises and setbacks.

Teachers and schools

Who are the teachers? They are the same professionals one would find in any school, but some will have taught in special schools, so they will have experience in working with children not in mainstream education.

Teachers and teaching assistants receive training in the Restorative Parenting programme in a similar way to the therapeutic parents who work in the homes. The school is obviously and necessarily a very different environment to the child's home, although there are some overlaps. The same support and advice mechanisms – that is, access to the clinical team, consultations and behaviour management advice – operate across both home and school. The teachers attend professionals' meetings and are fully engaged in monitoring and reporting the child's progress through the programme.

Notwithstanding the different routines and expectations which exist in school, there are also overlaps in the way behaviour is managed and a shared understanding of the children's strengths and abilities, as well as areas they find challenging. As we have explained previously, the children we work with have a greater than average need for consistency and are more susceptible to any actual or perceived uncertainties. Thus, there is a need to reduce as much as possible any potential contradictions in the way teachers and therapeutic parents interact with and manage a particular child.

In school, as in the home, it is important to consider the environment and its potential impact upon children. Just as we have explained how the home should be decorated and floors carpeted to achieve a warm but low-stimulus environment (see Chapter 3), the same needs to be considered in school, although the rooms do also have different purposes, which shapes their style and content to some extent.

A school needs to have spaces to display the children's work and to exhibit work plans and timetables. There are multi-sensory aspects to effective learning, so the children need to be able to use play and art materials. There is a role for music and the interactive use of information technology. All of this could, if not managed carefully in a way mindful of the children's sensitivities, create a chaotic sensory environment.

However, with proper organisation, the environment can still be ordered in a way that is itself therapeutic. Visual displays can be contained within delineated or framed areas, and play and art materials can be stored in cupboards, which means mess can be created and then cleared away, with things restored to how they were before. This is, in fact, an important aspect of many creative therapies in that there can be a sensory expression of emotions within a temporary and restorable context. In school, the children can benefit from experiencing different sensory activities in spaces which are then restored to the same order as before.

Another aspect of the school environment which can be supportive of the children's recovery is the value of routine. In any school, there are routines which are both explicit and implicit. The school day proceeds to a rhythm which is ordered and is expected and understood by everyone. This removes a great deal of uncertainty, and with it anxiety. If the children and teachers know where they are supposed to be and what they are supposed to be doing and at what time, it can become an almost unnoticed answer to many potential difficulties, and in that way immensely reassuring.

When referring to the value of order and routine, there is another issue worth mentioning that can occur when children are at school. Ofsted inspectors, who do have the right to make unannounced visits, need to be sensitive to the environment they are entering – be it an inspection of the home or the school – and to go about their work as unobtrusively as possible. Children can be told what their job is, so that they can be prepared for the visit.

The school day

Children should begin attending school as soon as possible after they come to live in the therapeutic home, which, in practice, will often mean the following day. They may have an introductory visit to look around and meet the teachers and fellow pupils, but a gap while they get used to the therapeutic care home and then go to school is likely to create additional problems. A child new to school might, though, have a shorter day than the other pupils, if needed, for one or two days, but it is important that her school day is, as soon as practicable, the same as that of all her fellow pupils.

As explained earlier, classrooms should also have timetables prominently displayed so that the children know where they will be and what they are doing, each day and at what time. This is because, in addition to the reassurance that order and routine can bring, some children who have suffered trauma come from families where life is chaotic, where there are few or no boundaries, and often parents' moods and attitudes and behaviour change arbitrarily toward their children.

Even unstructured time – playtime and lunch breaks – should have a structure. That is, the child should not have to think what she wants to do but be offered choices. These could include sports or arts clubs; playground games; or any number of things appropriate for the morning and afternoon breaks and lunch time after the children have eaten. Of course, in addition to activities in the school, these children are no different from others in their social needs, in that they enjoy activities outside the school like cubs, scouts and guides; a football club; or hockey.

Initially, some children may need to receive one-to-one teaching, with only limited engagement in wider classroom activities. Coming to a new school, the child is in an unfamiliar place and, at least in the early stages, many children do not like to interact with peers. Gradually, the children are encouraged and supported to move into classroom teaching, but even then, given the number of children in each home and the number attending mainstream school, these will be quite intimate classes of, say, a teacher with two or three children.

Children in the earlier stages of the Restorative Parenting programme tend to learn better in very small groups. They can be brought together with all pupils in one class later, and especially when a move to mainstream school is being contemplated.

Discipline

If a child is troublesome in class, there should be other rooms, or quiet learning areas, where it can be suggested she go. This should be a plain and unadorned room, with muted colours and soft furnishings, such as bean bags. Another such area could, for example, have a small table, a chair or settee, and a chalk board on the wall so that the child can write what she likes. It may also be a good idea for the walls in this room to be decorated with one picture or image that each child has in their own room – for example, an animal, a TV personality or a character from a book or film. This will make the room familiar to them. If it is found that the child starts to work in the room or prefers to stay there, she can be asked if she would like her books and pens (or whatever she was working on in the classroom) to be brought in so that she can continue there with what she was doing.

However, more serious behaviour problems may arise (indeed, given the background of pupils, they must be expected to arise). It is true that, in any school, children can act disruptively, sometimes seriously so and, in extreme cases, in mainstream education, the child could be excluded. However, with the type of child about whom this book is concerned, there should be no exclusions, as this would only reinforce the child's feeling of rejection. This is possible within the Restorative Parenting recovery programme because Halliwell Homes has its own schools. By the time a child is ready to move to a mainstream learning environment, her ability to self-manage and moderate her own emotional reactions should be such that exclusion is not required. However, if it were to happen, we recognise and understand the impact as being more pronounced and potentially more prolonged than it might be for another child. Our supportive response needs to be correspondingly greater.

Why a child reacts negatively may not be obvious or even easy to discern. The triggers may be hidden and revealed only by working with and getting to know the child. They could be a fleeting moment when the child is thinking about her mother; or something she has read in a book that provokes an unhappy memory. Sometimes there may be more obvious factors which impact upon a child's ability to regulate her behaviour, such as having learned that her mother is expecting a baby, which she intends to keep. The triggers are as different as the children and their backgrounds themselves, but what we do know is that many behaviour incidents, while apparently reactive to events in the moment, will also have links to that background.

While the children often come from dysfunctional families and will have experienced abuse – physical, verbal or sexual – or neglect, and sometimes two or more of these, this does not mean that they should not experience the kind of regime that children in mainstream schools know. For example, they should wear school uniform, and 100 per cent attendance should be expected. They should be required to call teachers 'Miss' and 'Sir'. This will prepare them for how they will find the regime in mainstream schools when the time comes for them to make the change to one. There are other ways in which the education of traumatised children is normalised. Similarly, the therapeutic parents should do what all parents do – they take their children to school, pick them up, or sometimes bring in their lunch. Therapeutic parents should be invited to parents' evenings to discuss the child's progress, but can also be called in if the child is exhibiting some kind of behaviour problem or experiencing difficulties with learning that cannot wait for a parents' evening.

Learning

Like life itself, school is replete with the potential for informal learning or learning by doing. In Chapter 2 we mentioned the boy who creates his own room – he chooses the furniture and decoration – and yet every so often destroys it. Yet in creating the room he has shown judgement, discernment, taste and an eye for design, colour and the placing of objects. He has done this by concentration and application. And, as we said, when that child comes up against a problem in one context, he has the memory of success in another context to indicate that the new problem is not insoluble.

Let's take the example of another kind of practical learning of the boy who, while his maths and numeracy are not the best, has excellent handiwork skills. So because he wants shelving and a wardrobe in his room, he is given the tools and materials needed to build them. But to achieve this he has also to read the instructions, which include taking measurements and using a tape measure, which are maths skills. This boy is thus exercising a skill and learning from it, and enjoying doing so.

Both children show a wide potential not only for the tasks they do but for what, in different ways, they learn from them.

Propensity to Learn measures

Before we discuss the child's move to mainstream education, it is necessary to explain the Propensity to Learn measures because, as will be seen, these are a critical element in assessing a child's readiness for such a move.

As we said above, restorative education is more than providing a good quality education, it is also about helping children to overcome the trauma they have experienced and re-build the ability to trust others. It contains five elements of children's propensity to learn. The elements are measured on a scale of one to five. Within each of the numerical ratings are three grades of a to c. These elements are an adaptation of the Restorative Parenting Recovery Index (see the Appendix), to which we referred in Chapter 2.

The measures monitor and record a child's emotional, social and behavioural progress throughout her time at school. They take into account age and level of maturity of the individual child. Their completion is vitally important in assessing the child's readiness for the next appropriate educational provision following her time at a school linked to the therapeutic home. Thus, they should be accorded high priority.

The Index is a measure of general progress, and so its completion should involve consideration and experience of the child in different contexts, taking part in a range of activities. The index is completed through a semi-structured interview with a member of the clinical team – in the same way that those in the home are completed.

In completing the measures, we do not include incidents which are clearly reactive to unusual events or circumstances. It is also worth remembering that the children with whom we are concerned do not tend to progress smoothly in their school lives, and thus ratings can become temporarily lower in certain areas as new emotional challenges are introduced through the curriculum.

When we think about the levels a child is achieving, practitioners will be aware of progress being made and areas of outstanding need. This helps to keep a focus on the tasks of restorative education that staff need to consider when teaching the curriculum.

Moving to the mainstream

The move to mainstream school is a very important one. It is known that the move from primary to secondary school can be a very testing one for many children, but children in the home will swap schools (mostly) at an earlier stage, so they could well have two moves – from home school to mainstream school and, later, the move from primary to secondary, like all children.

When that transition takes place, a teaching assistant from the home can accompany the child to the new school. However, so that this does not stigmatise the child or set her apart from her new fellow pupils, while the assistant is explicitly there for her, he can support the learning of other children in the class. This is because the teaching assistant should not be seen to be there just for the individual child, which then can single her out in the minds of the other children. At the very least, the teaching assistant is a friendly face for the child in what will be a completely new and very different (in so many ways) environment.

Effective communication between mainstream school teaching staff and the child's teaching assistant is crucial to the success of the transition. To give an example of how this communication can work effectively, take the case of the child who has had a disturbed night and has lost sleep. This may have been caused by some earlier incident at the home. That morning the teaching assistant collects her for school, but when he arrives, the child refuses to get out of the car. The teaching assistant goes into the school and speaks to the pastoral leader and says that in his opinion it would not be best for the child to attend school after such a night and in her current state of mind. The pastoral leader understands and agrees that it is best if that day the child does not attend school. He gives the teaching assistant school work for the child to complete at home so that progress through the curriculum is not missed.

The time when a child is ready to move from the home's school to the mainstream school will differ according to her rate of recovery and progress. This could be three to six months, but it could also be 12 to 18 months.

It may be thought that some children moving on to mainstream school will cause envy or resentment in those not leaving, or that a child leaving may taunt the other children because they have 'made it' and the others haven't. Not so: one child moving on is an encouragement for others to do so; it stimulates their ambitions and aspirations.

Moving to a mainstream school is important for all kinds of reasons. The child has made such encouraging progress that she can

move. In moving, very important steps in the educational ladder –
and not just in terms of learning – have been mounted. But this will
also say much about the emotional progress of the child through
the recovery programme; this can be a signal that foster care can be
started to be thought about.

Everyone's life is, as we say now, a journey. But, in fact, it is
one composed of many journeys, some of which are discrete but
which link with others later, or sometimes with earlier parts of the
journey. Children who have suffered trauma are no different. Their
journey through life is one which will have had far more disruption
and negative experiences than most. Along that way if they are lucky,
there will be people to help them. Teachers form an important part
in everyone's life, and education is a treasure that all can exploit. For
the child who has been traumatised, teachers and school are not only
about learning in the educational sense, but a critical part of their
recovery. Combined with the therapeutic environment in which they
live, education can equip these children to face the challenges of life
that all of us face, but with a strength that many of us did not have
to be helped to find in the same way.

CHAPTER 8

People at the Centre

Staff Consultation, Support and Values

Consultations

Staff consultation is a *sine qua non* of modern health and social care covering those of all ages and conditions, as it is for other public services and commercial organisations. Whether practice lives up to rhetoric is, at times, doubtful, but, with regard to children who have suffered trauma and rejection, because several different professionals will work with them, co-ordination must be integral to organisation practice, and consultation must be key to co-ordination. Consultations are important in that they provide a forum in which people who are actively caring for the child can collectively discuss issues and decide upon strategies which will help the child to progress.

An important aspect of restorative parenting is that a practitioner psychologist meets monthly for consultation with the practice team from each home. The consultation group comprises the child's key worker, the home's management team, and the child's teachers. Social workers can also attend. The consultations are led by clinical and educational psychologists who have substantial and varied experience of working with children.

The psychologist helps to empower the practice team by exploring avenues for change and eliciting possible solutions in response to identified challenges. This is not a matter of the 'expert' versus the 'non-expert' but rather a collaborative process of exploration, which uses re-framing, solution-focussed work, formulation sharing, information exchange and education.

In addition to consultations, children's key workers are interviewed monthly by a member of the clinical team to check the child's progress and complete the Restorative Parenting Recovery Index (see Chapter 2 and the Appendix). This process has the dual purpose of collating information and also further engaging the therapeutic practice team in the thoughtful application of the model.

In addition to the monthly consultations, all therapeutic parents have regular supervision which further helps to support and embed reflection and thinking about the practice of restorative parenting. To impact positively on the experience of the child, consultation, like specific clinical advice and training, must be consistently reflected in the day-to-day environment of the therapeutic home. It is not enough to have theoretical knowledge and understanding; to be effective, restorative parenting must inform thinking and practice at all levels.

Julie: how to learn by doing

Julie was 11 when she came to the home following a series of failed foster placements. Although a very intelligent girl, she had missed much of her schooling, and as a result she did not know how to read and write. She would often display destructive and violent behaviour in situations where she feared this inability might become apparent to other people. Julie had an interest in horses and riding, and this activity became part of her routine, which she enjoyed once or twice a week. Her riding always happened as planned, irrespective of her behaviour. The removal of the activity was never threatened as a sanction or offered as a reward. This was difficult for some newer members of the practice team to understand: why should Julie go riding if she had destroyed furniture, broken windows and even kicked and hit her teachers? How would she learn to behave differently if she was rewarded for such behaviour?

But an understanding of the programme answers such questions. Julie's behaviour masked her fears and insecurities, which manifested in a refusal to face her difficulties with reading. She was afraid of how people would see her and also afraid that the task of learning to read would prove too hard for her. Julie had very little self-confidence

– she expected failure and rejection at every turn. She had been biologically and psychologically programmed to survive in an anxious environment, and her behavioural reactions were naturally extreme. Given she had such a fundamental and profound lack of confidence, the removal of horse riding, the one thing she enjoyed, would have only reaffirmed what Julie expected and compounded her problems.

So instead, the riding continued, as did the learning of words to go with it. The words – 'horse', 'pony', 'stable', 'saddle', 'hay', 'straw', 'bridle', 'shoe' and words like them – were the first ones Julie learned to read and to spell. Her intelligence became obvious in the speed with which she learned to read and write once the initial barrier was overcome.

The Restorative Parenting programme teams and their members

In general, restorative parenting has a ratio of 20 members of the practice team working with six children in the homes, and all are therapeutic parents or therapeutic parent trainees. These proportions do not preclude or prevent a child developing a more intense relationship with one or more members of the practice team: the key factor is the child–adult relationship, which may develop in different (positive) ways, with different aspects, according to the individual relationship.

The clinical team comprises a clinical psychologist, a residential adviser to the clinical team, an assistant psychologist (who focuses on audit and evaluation), and two educational psychologists to manage consultations with the staff team, as well as undertaking assessments. In addition, consultant therapists from outside can be brought in if required to undertake specific therapeutic work with individual children. This intervention is not, however, routine, as the therapeutic parent within the home environment is the means by which the recovery programme is delivered.

The key worker spends individual time with the child regularly to find out how things are going, and to look at any issues or concerns.

This input is generally informal with no fixed agenda, but it could also include, for example, life story work (see Chapter 2), address contact, or provide advice on sleep management.

Supporting staff

It is true that some children become skilled at identifying what may hurt a staff member – for example, making negative remarks when the staff member has suffered a bereavement – but, at root, this is about the child driving the carer away and is connected to the child's own damaged psychology, which will be connected to the child's own history.

This means that counselling for staff should be available when required, and should be confidential so that it is not shared with managers. Indeed, staff should be encouraged to take up the benefits of counselling, rather than wait until they feel the need to do so, as this is a means of managing any emotional issue which may have an impact on a staff member's availability to a child.

Counselling may not be about what has happened in the home with other staff or the relationship between child and worker but may be needed for personal issues, like bereavement or marital problems. Some staff may not need counselling for this, and there will also be staff who are especially resilient and have developed personal mechanisms to cope with professional matters, which will often obviate the need for them to seek counselling. However, the resource is available to all, and its use should be regarded positively and should be encouraged at all levels of the organisation.

It is important to consider the ability of therapeutic parents to respond appropriately to challenging situations, both at the outset when they first join the organisation, but also on an ongoing basis. The emotional stability and availability of the therapeutic parent are important aspects of the child's lived experience and one which is attended to carefully and continuously.

Relationships with other professionals

Apart from staff at the home and teachers, there are other types of professional with whom a child may have contact, for example the police, GPs, inspectors and social workers.

Police

A positive relationship with the local police can be a valuable asset to the home. Proactive liaison with the police can prevent a number of potential problems from escalating and, if issues do arise, these can often be addressed more quickly and productively if good relationships between the home and the police are already in place.

Children who come into the programme, especially those who have experienced a succession of failed placements, are likely to present behaviours warranting police involvement. Absconding and making allegations are the two main areas where this happens and where good communication and information sharing can help achieve the most positive outcome for the child.

The police can have a very important role in keeping children safe, and within the Restorative Parenting programme it is important to try to help the children to understand this, but also to recognise, in partnership with the local liaison officer, that the police do have a bigger job to do.

Within other, what might be termed more traditional, residential care settings, it is not uncommon for staff to call in the police when there are incidents of vandalism, minor assaults or destruction of property when for the same 'offence' no parent would involve the police. This type of police involvement, as punishment or sanction, has little to do with meeting the child's needs and therefore has no place within the Restorative Parenting programme.

A key part of therapeutic parenting is the effective management of behaviour using the positive behaviour support model described earlier. A therapeutic parent who says 'Katie punched me and I'm calling the police' is displaying a non-therapeutic thought process. This is because such a reaction is based on the assumption that the child's behaviour was deliberate, malicious and targeted. It assumes, too, that reporting it to the police – a punitive consequence – will help to ensure the behaviour will not happen again. In reality, the opposite is true in a child who expects rejection and seeks proof of this expectation at every turn.

Reactively involving the police also shifts the responsibility for dealing with the behaviour from the therapeutic parent to the police. And, not least, it confirms for the child her own sense of worthlessness, so she sees the reporting as a consequence of who she is. Thus, rather than going to the police, the need is for the therapeutic parent to understand the behaviour, make non-blaming attributions and to manage situations confidently and effectively, making use of the extensive support available.

To be effective, the therapeutic programme must instil the belief in children that therapeutic parents are competent and capable, that they are people who can be relied upon to provide safety. Police involvement due to challenging behaviour, if it is ever necessary, is likely to be damaging to the children's sense of safety and security, and for that reason it is always viewed as a serious action – a step of last resort in the face of a severe and otherwise unmanageable risk.

General practitioners and health care staff

General practitioners and other health care staff are professionals whom children are likely to see routinely for health checks and in relation to common childhood ailments.

A therapeutic parent, like any other parent, potentially has a significant contribution to make to the process of a child being diagnosed with a chronic condition (for example, asthma), or other illness. Children cannot refer themselves to GPs, and in making a diagnosis a GP is often at least partially reliant on parental descriptions of what ails the child – chronic indigestion, stomach upset, breathing difficulties, and so on. ADHD is probably the most common example where parent and carer reports are a critical part of the diagnostic process. While on many occasions this information may be correct, at others, especially when provided by parents whose own lives are, at least, disturbed and, at worse, chaotic, it may be misleading. In taking the child to appointments with GPs and other health professionals, the therapeutic parent must know the child well enough to be able to provide clear and accurate information. He must also be conscious of his responsibilities in this respect – children who progress through the care system often prompt medical concerns and receive tests and investigations on the basis of carer concerns which may be overstated.

One area where the therapeutic parents need to be particularly careful is when describing the child's emotional and behavioural difficulties. All of the children referred to the programme meet the threshold for referral to the local Child and Adolescent Mental Health Service (CAMHS). If the GP is not made aware of the nature of the programme, then a referral can easily be made, which can lead to confusion because the child then enters a new system dealing with the same problem which led to the child being placed within the Restorative Parenting programme. Thus, it is also important that there is a good relationship between CAMHS and the home so that, if that referral is made, the CAMHS team can be assured that the programme itself is working with the child on her emotional and behavioural issues.

Inspectors

Ofsted inspectors, and sometimes officials from local authorities, can make surprise visits to children's homes. Every effort should be made to ensure that any visit causes only minimal disruption. This may not always be practical, and homes must trust that inspectors are experienced, practical people, who can manage situations sensitively with awareness of the therapeutic environment. If an inspector wishes to speak to a child, the child must be willing and able to do so, and the conversation must take place somewhere the child feels comfortable. Some children may not feel able to talk to an inspector without being accompanied by a familiar adult to support her. This can sometimes cause difficulties if the inspector would prefer to speak to the child alone. In these situations, we would encourage and support the child to do so, perhaps suggesting that the meeting take place in school or as part of an activity.

Planned professional visits should always be managed carefully, as they can bring an unwelcoming and disruptive formality to a home. Wherever possible, all meetings involving groups of professionals should be held away from the home. However, social workers should be able to meet children in the home, because that is the child's home, and if the children were living with their families that is what would happen.

Unfortunately, at times, inspectors can find shortcomings in the home. In a well-run home these will often be minor and temporary, but particularly when working with children who make regular allegations, even minor lapses can attract intense scrutiny. Of course, it is quite right that this happens if there is any concern that practice within the home may be in any way injurious to a child's welfare. But, putting such obvious concerns aside, an administrative fault or minor error within the home's regulatory management does not say anything about that which is key within the home: the strength of the relationships between staff and children. These relationships are the bedrock of the children's welfare, security, safety and recovery. Children do not live within a set of quality standards, and an overly legalistic attitude on the part of some inspectors as to what the letter of particular regulations say is sometimes at odds with this – and the loss is the children's.

Social workers

Each child will have a social worker. The social worker is responsible for monitoring the child's progress while in the care of the home, and some children may develop a close relationship with their social worker. However, it is nevertheless the case that, too often, social workers come and go – they leave the local authority, their caseloads are switched, they are promoted, or they leave for other reasons. Not only do they go out of the child's life – a life where very likely too many people have come and gone – but they will be replaced by another social worker, and there is no assurance that that person, too, may not, after a while, disappear. Both therapeutic parents and teachers, who are likely to be much more of a constant presence in a child's life, need to be aware of the negative effect this may have on a child and how it may affect her behaviour or, in the case of the school, her ability to concentrate.

Social workers, like other professionals who need to visit the child, should try not to turn up unannounced and disrupt what the child is doing. Sensitivity is required on the social worker's part.

The child's family

Restorative parenting is about providing replacement parenting for a child. But when there is contact between child and parent, restorative parenting should not be seen to be in competition with birth families – there should be partnership.

However, it remains a lamentable fact that even sometimes where contact is possible, it is too often unreliable: the parent will turn up late or not at all. The child who is separated from her parents may have confused expectations of them, and disrupted contact can easily exacerbate and compound existing anxieties. Whatever the child may like to believe about this, ultimately he or she will fear that the parent does not want to see her and experience a further sense of rejection. Thus, the need must be to ensure that the expectation of contact once set can be realistically met as far as the parent is concerned. Such children have often experienced too much inconsistency and disappointment from too many people, even professionals, for them to suffer this at the hands of someone as significant as a parent. It is another example, too, of the inconsistency of adults that blights too many children's lives.

Children need the support of adults outside the home and, if no parental contact is possible, someone else may be able to step in. This could be another relative (like a grandparent or aunt or uncle) or, if no relative is reliably available, a therapeutic aunt or uncle. These latter may be former staff, who have expressed a wish to maintain continuing contact with a child, or occasionally individuals recruited as volunteers.

Contact may be a challenging experience for a parent if a child shows anger or disinhibited behaviour. The parent may see this as negative, whereas this may be a communication: as if the child is saying 'Why am I not at home?' and 'Why is my mum not caring for me?' The parent should be helped to see that it is positive that the child feels able to express herself in this way.

Contact is not only about maintaining a relationship with a parent or parents which may have later positive repercussions, but it is also about identity and who the child is. It can act as a counterweight to fantasy, where a child may believe (and say) that he or she was abandoned, had been taken from the family, or that the parents are unavailable, even dead, or other such imaginary life situations as she entertains.

Family contact often takes place using charity or local authority contact centres or, more informally, in a park or café or at bowling, or perhaps another activity centre. The Restorative Parenting programme also has its own contact centre, and other agencies may have this facility. Wherever the contact is, it should be child-friendly and allow parent and child as natural an interaction as possible in a non-institutional environment.

Contact sometimes needs to be formally supervised because of something which the parent may say to the child, or the way he or she may act toward the child. This raises a potential conflict of roles for the therapeutic parent, which will require sensitivity and care. It may also be that the therapeutic parent may have to curtail the contact if the parent introduces ideas about, or talks to the child about, things that are clearly distressing to the child. An example might be that a parent could become upset and blame the child for the upset caused to the family, which may be a disguised but all too obvious reference to the child having disclosed abuse.

Telephone contact can be particularly problematic, requiring careful management and the setting of boundaries. For younger children, such contact is often difficult, and it needs to be quite short and not too frequent to be of value to them.

Values

No home will succeed, no child will ever be helped and no staff member will be able to do their job to the best of their ability unless staff are motivated by strong and consistent values. These should not only motivate them but permeate the working environment.

Values within restorative parenting are about making positive attributions about children and ensuring that all actions contribute to their psychological health and wellbeing. But what are these values? The one which underlies all others, and the work, is that the child is a person entitled to be treated with respect and dignity, whatever her behaviour. She is a child first and foremost and can never be seen in terms of her problems. Thus, her problems should be seen as needs. From this stems another value – the recognition of the child's potential, and a focus on what she can do, not what it is assumed she cannot do.

Staff work on the basis of informed optimism. This is not about a cheerful disregard of the obstacles, which can be formidable, but being focussed on what the child's needs are and a commitment to that child, and being positive that she can change and progress.

Our values have to be an active, practical expression of how we view children – how we view the individual child – and what we can do for them and with them. Alas, workers can too easily fall into the trap of seeing children negatively and thus dismissively, which rebounds negatively on how the child is dealt with and the prospects for her recovery.

Take the example of Mark, aged ten, who had engaged in incest with a younger sibling and had been placed with a foster carer. At a planning meeting, a fostering social worker said: 'If Mark was a car and the foster carer was the prospective buyer, Mark would be the last one left on the forecourt.' Such a dismissive attitude has no place in any public service, but especially one which works with very damaged and undervalued children, whose own estimation of themselves will be low. If an organisational culture or a staff member has low expectations of a child, then outcomes will be low. Moreover, a staff member who speaks like that to other staff cannot help but communicate that feeling, if not explicitly stating it, to the children with whom he works.

A precept by Gandhi (2001) is one which should guide staff:

Keep your thoughts positive, because your thoughts become your words. Keep your words positive, because your words become your behaviour. Keep your behaviour positive, because your behaviour becomes your habits. Keep your habits positive, because your habits become your values. Keep your values positive, because your values become your destiny.

RESTORATIVE PARENTING RECOVERY INDEX[1]

Introduction

The Restorative Parenting Recovery Index is both a marker of a child's progress and a guide through the therapeutic journey.

- Each of the five indexes is rated on a scale of 1 to 5. Within each numerical rating, there are three gradings of a to c.

- Each child is initially assessed against the Progress and Development Index within the first four weeks of placement and thereafter on a monthly basis.

- Ratings are discussed and agreed by a child's key worker and a member of the clinical team.

In completing the index, the following key points should always be considered:

- the general behaviour and emotional presentation of the child over the last four weeks rather than a focus on acute instances

- the age and level of maturity of the child

- any significant changes or events impacting on the child during the preceding four weeks – this can be personal, interpersonal or environmental.

---

1   The Restorative Parenting Recovery Index has now been updated.

1. Completing the Restorative Parenting Recovery Index

1.1 The Restorative Parenting Recovery Index is the main way in which a child's progress through the therapeutic programme is monitored and recorded. It is crucial that the index is completed carefully and correctly to provide a reliable and valid measure. Proper completion of the index is a key aspect of the therapeutic programme and should be given a high priority.

1.2 The index is completed by recording observations of the child's presentation and behaviour in different settings and their reactions and responses to different situations and challenges.

1.3 Therapeutic parents make the main contribution to determining the scores for each child because of their direct experience and knowledge. The scores are discussed with a member of the clinical team as this adds to the reliability of the index.

1.4 When completing the index, consider the age and the level of maturity of the child or young person. The rating process should reflect what can reasonably be expected of a child at that developmental stage or level. For example, a child of five may have a good level of ability in terms of self-care, whilst still needing a high degree of adult support and supervision. However, this level of dependency on adults is age appropriate and so should not attract a low rating as it would with an older child.

1.5 Index ratings are meant to reflect a child's general progress through the programme. Therefore behaviours and emotions which are clearly reactive to unusual events or circumstances should not be included in the rating process.

1.6 Most children will not progress smoothly through the programme, and their ratings on the index will sometimes become temporarily lower in certain areas as new emotional challenges are addressed.

2. Rating the indexes

2.1 The highest rating on each index is 5c. The lowest rating is 1a. When considering a child's presentation in relation to the index, the first decision is the numerical rating. Remember, the ratings are designed to reflect the child's general presentation and should not rely on single examples of behaviour.

2.2 The a, b or c level within each numerical rating reflects the extent to which the child or young person has achieved that level of functioning. It is unlikely that a child who has only just begun to display the ability described would achieve a rating higher than 'a'. A 'c' rating is given when the level of function/ability described by the numerical rating is well established and expressed throughout all of the contexts the child usually encounters.

2.3 The following pages briefly describe each index and offer some guidance regarding each rating to help you decide what level a child is at. There is also space on the score sheet to make your own notes on what features of the child's presentation you considered in arriving at a particular rating. Over time, these notes will help you to compile a more detailed index and manual guide to recording a child's progress through a Restorative Parenting programme.

3. Not just an index

3.1 The Restorative Parenting Recovery Index is a key part of the therapeutic programme. An understanding of restorative parenting should inform all levels of practice. The ratings are not stand-alone measures, and the index should reflect the general presentation and progress of a child through the programme.

3.2 Therapeutic parents should become familiar with the information in this book. By thinking about the levels a child is achieving at each stage of the programme, practitioners will be aware of progress being made and areas of outstanding need. This helps to keep a focus on the tasks of therapeutic parenting and provide an overall direction which everyone in your team can work towards. Remember, restorative parenting is about more than providing good quality care, it is about helping children to overcome trauma and re-build the ability to trust. The Restorative Parenting Recovery Index is a key part of achieving that goal, and this index is both a marker of a child's progress and a guide through the therapeutic journey.

SELF-CARE (INDEX 1)

5. Can the child care for him or herself?

   In terms of looking after themselves in context by demonstrating sufficient social awareness to stay safe on a day-to-day basis without the need for unusual or age-inappropriate levels of intervention.

   a=rarely, b=sometimes, c=mostly

4. The child is developing his/her own personal styles and tastes, and with gentle assertiveness.

   Expressing opinions and showing an ability to make and communicate choices appropriately.

   a=rarely, b=sometimes, c=mostly

3. The child takes care in his/her appearance and achievements.

   Makes good use of learning opportunities, is self-aware, makes positive self-references.

   a=rarely, b=sometimes, c=mostly

2. The child allows others to offer care with his/her appearance, health and hygiene, and is aware of the problems which can occur if this is refused.

   The child may at times pretend to clean but is accepting of advice and willing to attend appropriate appointments with encouragement.

   a=rarely, b=sometimes, c=mostly

1. The child needs basic survival care.

   In terms of maintaining personal hygiene, regulating food intake and awareness of basic environmental dangers.

   a=mostly, b=sometimes, c=rarely

FORMING RELATIONSHIPS AND ATTACHMENTS (INDEX 2)

5. The child has developed the capacity to make trusting and lasting relationships, in a family, a peer group or cultural group.

   Has the child developed new and appropriate (non-damaging) social relationships which are consistent and stable over time?

   a=rarely, b=sometimes, c=mostly

4. The child has developed the capacity to make close relationships (e.g. at school, in the home, or at a club based outside the home).

   The child is initiating contact and interaction, which is building relationships that are positive and involve a reciprocal element.

   a=rarely, b=sometimes, c=mostly

3. The child is forming a relationship with one residential or foster carer.

   Expresses a consistent interest in the whereabouts and wellbeing of a particular person and responds in a more positive way to them.

   a=rarely, b=sometimes, c=mostly

2. The child is able to make a relationship with one 'safe' attachment figure (e.g. very young child, an older adult or pet).

   The child shows consistent acceptance of the relationship and demonstrates an emotional response. For example, welcoming or saying goodbye to the attachment figure.

   a=rarely, b=sometimes, c=mostly

1. The child has no known relationships or is emotionally frozen/closed.

   The child is unresponsive on an emotional level and shows no concern or interest in other people as individuals. This is more likely to be observed during the early stage of placement, but may occur briefly later on. The child generally avoids social interaction and does not take part in shared activities, although there may be small exceptions.

   a=mostly, b=sometimes, c=rarely

SELF-PERCEPTION (INDEX 3)

5. The child is aware of their own strengths and weaknesses, with a positive self-image.

   Is able to reflect upon situations and challenges and communicate doubts while maintaining an overall positive view of self. In addition, setbacks are managed without major distress.

   a=rarely, b=sometimes, c=mostly

4. The child is aware of how others see them and their own ability to change.

   The child can compare themselves with others in a realistic way, and is able to take account of feedback and manage constructive criticism without becoming upset.

   a=rarely, b=sometimes, c=mostly

3. The child has a sense of self mainly governed by others.

   Behaviour is variable and only contained when supervision is active and visible.

   a=mostly, b=sometimes, c=rarely

2. The child has a low or unrealistic perception of self – for example, showing signs of self-neglect or inflated self-perception.

   Takes little interest in self-care, clothes and appearance in general, or the child may be obsessive about certain aspects of presentation. The child may make up stories about experience or abilities to present themselves and their background in an unrealistic light.

   a=mostly, b=sometimes, c=rarely

1. The child sees themselves as unimportant, useless or hateful.

   The child does not expect basic care and may be confused by provision of regular food and clean clothes – is this for me? The child may also make very self-critical comments.

   a=mostly, b=sometimes, c=rarely

SELF-MANAGEMENT AND SELF-AWARENESS (INDEX 4)

5. The child can predict or accept negative events and can attempt to manage, learn from and move on from these.

    This level will also be linked to the child's ability to accept positive praise. Basically, it refers to the child being able to cope with and manage significant setbacks and disappointments without being overwhelmed and to demonstrate learning as a result.

    a=rarely, b=sometimes, c=mostly

4. The child is generally able to manage the highs and lows of everyday life and take responsibility for actions.

    The child is able to respond to situations appropriately. They may express annoyance or disappointment, but without excessive emotion or behavioural reactions. Similarly, the child can deal with exciting times, achievement and successes without over-reacting. The child is able to recognise and understand the consequences of their own behaviour. They understand restorative justice and accept appropriate sanctions.

    a=rarely, b=sometimes, c=mostly

3. The child can manage some problem situations but needs support from others and a highly structured environment.

    This level will apply to many children in the residential programme. In practice it should include consideration of the child's ability to accept advice and guidance. Also includes the extent to which the child has a realistic view of their own capabilities.

    a=rarely, b=sometimes, c=mostly

2. The child is unable to manage their behaviour and has poor impulse control. The child is self-focussed and has little or no awareness of their behaviours on others or the needs of others.

    This doesn't mean the child has extreme reactions, but that they do find it very hard not to react to anything going on around them. The child is not concerned about what other people think. Can be sulky and defiant in public situations. Group activities can be disrupted.

a=mostly, b=sometimes, c=rarely

1. The child's emotions and behaviour are generally dominated by small setbacks, disappointments or the need for instant gratification.

The child cannot manage without instant gratification – they cannot wait or defer reactions. A child at this level may present as very unstable and be prone to frequent, sometimes extreme, variations in mood. They may feel justified in behaviour, at the time and afterwards, even if it has caused major problems for others.

a=mostly, b=sometimes, c=rarely

EMOTIONAL COMPETENCE (INDEX 5)

5. The child is able to understand and accept their own feelings and the feelings of others, and is able to respond appropriately to both.

   The child has self-awareness and reacts consistently and in a considerate way to most situations, having awareness of other people's needs and feelings.

   a=rarely, b=sometimes, c=mostly

4. The child can understand, control and manage a range of their own emotions.

   The child is able to manage emotional and behavioural reactions, including understanding context and explanation. They can express emotions appropriately.

   a=rarely, b=sometimes, c=mostly

3. The child has knowledge of a range of emotions and is beginning to match appropriate emotions to context.

   The emotion expressed is appropriate to the event and context, and the child is able to limit their emotional expression.

   a=rarely, b=sometimes, c=mostly

2. The child too often misinterprets the emotions of others as well as their own emotional responses.

   Can be mood related, but the child is prone to over-reaction and has difficulty understanding context – they may expect things to always be the same. The child may cry, become angry or run away very easily in response to minor triggers.

   a=mostly, b=sometimes, c=rarely

1. The child is unable to understand or control their own emotions or has unexplainable changes of mood and/or blames others for their own moods.

   The child presents as very volatile and/or easily upset, often with no clear triggers. They may make unjustified accusations of blame or mistreatment.

   a=mostly, b=sometimes, c=rarely

REFERENCES

Aynsley-Green, A. (2005) 'Understanding opportunities for improving the lives of children and young people.' YoungMinds Annual Lecture, 10 November.

Bateson, P., Gluckman, P. and Hanson, M. (2014) 'The biology of developmental plasticity and the predictive adaptive response hypothesis.' *The Journal of Physiology, 592*, 11, 2357–2368.

Beckett, C. (2002) *Human Growth and Development*. London: Sage.

Bjork, D. W. (1997) *B. F. Skinner: A Life*. Washington DC: American Psychological Association.

Bowlby, J. (1969) *Attachment and Loss: Vol. 1. Loss*. New York: Basic Books.

Cairns, K. (2002) *Attachment, Trauma and Resilience: Therapeutic Caring for Children*. London: BAAF Adoption and Fostering.

Carroll, J. E., Gruenewald, T. L., Taylor, S. E., Janicki-Deverts, D. *et al.* (2013) 'Childhood abuse, parental warmth, and adult multisystem biological risk in the Coronary Artery Risk Development in Young Adults Study.' *Proceedings of the National Academy of Sciences of the USA, 110*, 42, 17149–17153.

Connor, T., Sclare, I., Dunbar, D. and Elliffe, J. (1985) 'Making a life story book.' *Adoption and Fostering, 9*, 2.

Coram BAAF (2015) *Statistics: England*. Available at www.baaf.org.uk/res/statengland, accessed 9 February 2016.

Daws, D. (1993) *Through the Night: Helping Parents and Sleepless Infants*. London: Free Association Books.

Dockar-Drysdale, B. (1990) *The Provision of Primary Experience: Winnicottian Work with Children and Adolescents*. London: Free Association Books.

Evans, G. W. and Kim, P. (2012) 'Childhood poverty and young adults' allostatic load: The mediating role of childhood cumulative risk exposure.' *Psychological Science, 23*, 9, 979–983.

Felitti, V. J., Anda, R. F., Nordenberg, D., Williamson, D. F. *et al.* (1998) 'Relationship of childhood abuse and household dysfunction to many of the leading causes of death in adults: The Adverse Childhood Experiences (ACE) Study.' *American Journal of Preventative Medicine, 14*, 4, 245–258.

Gandhi, M. (2001) Quoted in T. Gold (ed.) *Open Your Mind, Open Your Life: A Book of Eastern Wisdom*. Riverside, NJ: Andrews McMeel Publishing.

Howe, D. (2000) 'Attachment Theory.' In M. Davies (ed.) *The Blackwell Encyclopaedia of Social Work*. Oxford: Blackwell.

Koomar, J. A. (2009) 'Trauma- and attachment-informed sensory integration assessment and intervention.' *Sensory Integration, 32*, 4.

Lamb, M. (2005) 'Attachments, social networks and developmental contexts.' *Human Development, 48*, 108–112.

Larkin, P. (2015) *High Windows.* London: Faber and Faber.

Lewis, M. (2005) 'The child and its family: The social network model.' *Human Development, 48,* 8–27.

Macdonald, G. and Millen, S. (2012) *Therapeutic Approaches to Social Work in Residential Child Care Settings: Literature Review.* London: Social Care Institute for Excellence.

Maginn, C. (2006) 'Pillar talk.' *Community Care,* 16–22 March.

Maier, H. W. (1981) 'Essential Components in Care and Treatment Environments for Children.' In F. Ainsworth and L. C. Fulcher (eds) *Group Care for Children: Concepts and Issues.* London: Tavistock.

Maier, S. F. and Seligman, M. E. (1976) 'Learned helplessness: Theory and evidence.' *Journal of Experimental Psychology, 105,* 1.

Perry, B. (1999) 'The Memories of States: How the Brain Receives and Retrieves Traumatic Experience.' In J. Goodwin and R. Attias (eds) *Splintered Reflections: Images of the Body in Trauma.* New York: Basic Books.

Pughe, B. and Philpot, T. (2007) *Living Alongside a Child's Recovery: Therapeutic Parenting with Traumatized Children.* London: Jessica Kingsley Publishers.

Robinson, C., Aston-Donley, L. and Brown, A. (Undated) 'Introducing Restorative Parenting.' (paper submitted for publication).

Rose, R. and Philpot, T. (2004) *The Child's Own Story: Life Story Work with Traumatised Children.* London: Jessica Kingsley Publishers.

Rosenström, T., Jylha, P., Pulkki-Råback, L., Holma, M. *et al.* (2015) 'Long-term personality changes and predictive adaptive responses after depressive episodes.' *Evolution and Human Behavior, 36,* 337–344.

Rymaszewska, J. and Philpot, T. (2005) *Reaching the Vulnerable Child: Therapy with Traumatized Children.* London: Jessica Kingsley Publishers.

Seligman, M. E. P. (1972) 'Learned helplessness.' *Annual Review of Medicine, 23,* 1, 407–412.

Seligman, M. E. P. (2002) *Authentic Happiness: Using the New Positive Psychology to Realise Your Potential for Deep Fulfilment.* London: Nicholas Brealey.

Shonkoff, J. P. and Garner, A. S. (2012) 'The lifelong effects of early childhood adversity and toxic stress.' *Pediatrics, 129,* 1, 232–246.

Spencer, J., Clearfield, M., Corbetta, D., Ulrich, B., Buchanan, P. and Schoner, G. (2006) 'Moving toward a grand theory of development: In memory of Esther Thelen.' *Child Development, 72,* 1327–1346.

van der Kolk, B. A. (2003) 'The neurobiology of childhood trauma and abuse.' *Child and Adolescent Psychiatric Clinics, 12,* 293–317.

van der Kolk, B. (2014) *The Body Keeps the Score: Mind, Brain and Body in the Transformation of Trauma.* London: Allen Lane.

Wolf, M., van Doorn, G. S. and Weissing, F. J. (2008) 'Evolutionary emergence of responsive and unresponsive personalities.' *Proceedings of the National Academy of Sciences, 105,* 41, 15825–15830.

ABOUT THE AUTHORS

Dr Chris Robinson is a clinical psychologist who has spent over 20 years working with children and families in a variety of settings, from acute mental health services and community-based CAMHS to family law. He has always had a keen interest in helping looked-after children through understanding their experiences and therapeutic needs. He is a well-regarded speaker and teaches on a number of topics related to child mental health. More recently he has begun to write and publish his work.

Terry Philpot is a writer and journalist. He has written and edited 19 books on subjects ranging from adoption to sex offending; and from learning disability to the voluntary sector. His most recent books are *31 London Cemeteries to Visit Before You Die* (2013); and *Beside the Seaside: Brighton's Places and Its People* (2015). He is also the author of 19 entries in the *Oxford Dictionary of National Biography*.

He has contributed to a wide range of publications, including *The Independent* and *The Guardian*. He is a regular writer and reviewer for *The Tablet*. He is a trustee of three charities and has won several awards for journalism.

ABOUT HALLIWELL HOMES

Halliwell Homes is a social enterprise offering clinically informed practice within residential homes and school settings within the Greater Manchester area. Its objective is to enhance the psychological wellbeing of children within the looked-after system.

Established in 1998 as a traditional children's home, in 2010 its directors Karen Mitchell-Mellor and Andrew Constable recognised that working with this model of child care lacked a professional focus on the clinical aspects of parenting later identified as restorative parenting, which resulted in unsatisfactory outcomes for most children parented by the state.

Over the last few years a journey has been undertaken, which has involved working with partners and developing a team to review clinically and adjust all elements of the organisation's activity to create a positive psychological impact on all children. Working with local authorities, educationalists and health workers, this process has transformed Halliwell's practice and the experience for the children for whom it cares.

Halliwell's programme is communicated through nationally delivered continuous professional development (CPD) training offered to fellow professionals within the looked-after system, offering formally accredited training courses, and publishing papers and books. Halliwell also offers consultancy work supporting the approach outlined in this book to education, residential, health and social services.

Halliwell's vision is to create a professionally qualified therapeutic parenting and education workforce able to offer restorative parenting to meet the needs of children to re-establish psychological wellbeing into adulthood. Looking into the future, it hopes to develop further its understanding of the organisational system best suited to supporting the task and applying the knowledge base through a suitably qualified and supervised workforce empowered through a programme, of experiential-based learning.

As part of Halliwell's continued development of the programme, its next step is to seek to work collaboratively to establish studies of outcomes in the UK and a national training centre seeking to develop further and validate the skills necessary to develop fully the role of the therapeutic parent.

Contact: enquiries@Halliwellhomes.co.uk; website: www.Halliwellhomes.co.uk

INDEX

A Guide to Therapeutic Child Care
What You Need to Know to Create a Healing Home
Ruth Emond, Laura Steckley and Autumn Roesch-Marsh

Paperback: £15.99 / $24.95

ISBN: 978 1 84905 401 0

eISBN: 978 0 85700 769 8

240 pages

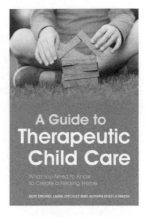

A Guide to Therapeutic Child Care provides an easy to read explanation of the secrets that lie behind good quality therapeutic child care.

It describes relevant theories, the 'invisible' psychological challenges that children will often struggle with and how to develop a nurturing relationship and build trust. Combining advice with practical strategies, the book also provides specific guidance on how to create safe spaces (both physical and relational) and how to aid the development of key social or emotional skills for children which may be lacking as a result of early trauma.

Written with input from foster carers, the book is an ideal guide for residential child care workers, foster carers, kinship carers, social workers and new adoptive parents.

Ruth Emond works part time in the School of Applied Social Science, University of Stirling and is a social worker and play therapist providing therapy to children and parents who have experienced trauma. **Laura Steckley** works at the University of Strathclyde as part of the School of Social Work and Social Policy and the Centre of Excellence for Looked After Children in Scotland. **Autumn Roesch-Marsh** is a qualified social worker with experience of working with children in residential and community settings. Autumn currently works at the University of Edinburgh as a Lecturer in Social Work.

Therapeutic Residential Care for Children and Youth
Developing Evidence-Based International Practice
Edited by James K. Whittaker, Jorge F. del Valle and Lisa Holmes

Paperback: £27.99 / $45.00
ISBN: 978 1 84905 792 9
eISBN: 978 0 85700 833 6
392 pages

Therapeutic Residential Care For Children and Youth takes a fresh look at therapeutic residential care as a powerful intervention in working with the most troubled children who need intensive support.

Featuring contributions from distinguished international contributors, it critically examines current research and innovative practice and addresses the key questions: how does it work, what are its critical 'active ingredients' and does it represent value for money? The book covers a broad spectrum of established and emerging approaches pioneered around with world, with contributors from the USA, Canada, Scandinavia, Spain, Australia, Israel and the UK offering a mix of practice and research exemplars. The book also looks at the research relating to critical issues for child welfare service providers: the best time to refer children to residential care, how children can be helped to make the transition into care, the characteristics of children entering and exiting care, strategies for engaging families as partners, how the substantial cost of providing intensive is best measured against outcomes, and what research and development challenges will allow therapeutic residential care to be rigorously compared with its evidence-based community-centered alternatives. Importantly, the volume also outlines how to set up and implement intensive child welfare services, considering how transferable they are, how to measure success and value for money, and the training protocols and staffing needed to ensure that a programme is effective.

This comprehensive volume will enable child welfare professionals, researchers and policymakers to develop a refined understanding of the potential of therapeutic residential care, and to identify the highest and best uses of this intensive and specialized intervention.

Therapeutic Residential Care for Children and Young People
An Attachment and Trauma-Informed Model for Practice
Susan Barton, Rudy Gonzalez and Patrick Tomlinson

Paperback: £22.99 / $39.95
ISBN: 978 1 84905 255 9
eISBN: 978 0 85700 538 0
288 pages

Children and young people in care who have been traumatized need a therapeutic environment where they can heal and which meets their emotional and developmental needs.

This book provides a model of care for traumatized children and young people, based on theory and practice experience pioneered at the Lighthouse Foundation, Australia. The authors explain the impact of trauma on child development, drawing on psychodynamic, attachment and neurobiological trauma theories. The practical aspects of undertaking therapeutic care are then outlined, covering everything from forming therapeutic relationships to the importance of the home environment and daily routines. The book considers the totality of the child's experience at the individual, group, organization and community levels and argues that attention to all of these is essential if the child is to achieve wellness. Case material from both children and carers are used throughout to illustrate both the impact of trauma and how children have been helped to recovery through therapeutic care.

This book will provide anyone caring for traumatized children and young people in a residential setting with both the understanding and the practical knowledge to help children recover. It will be essential reading for managers and decision-makers responsible for looked after children, child care workers such as residential and foster carers, youth workers, social workers, mental health workers and child welfare academics.